Business Guides on the Go

"Business Guides on the Go" presents cutting-edge insights from practice on particular topics within the fields of business, management, and finance. Written by practitioners and experts in a concise and accessible form the series provides professionals with a general understanding and a first practical approach to latest developments in business strategy, leadership, operations, HR management, innovation and technology management, marketing or digitalization. Students of business administration or management will also benefit from these practical guides for their future occupation/careers.

These Guides suit the needs of today's fast reader.

Jörg Middendorf

Solution-focused Business Coaching

A Guide for Individual and Team Coaching

Jörg Middendorf
BCO
Frechen, Germany

Translation from the German language edition: "Lösungsorientiertes Coaching" by Jörg Middendorf, © Springer Fachmedien Wiesbaden GmbH, ein Teil von Springer Nature 2019. Published by Springer Fachmedien Wiesbaden. All Rights Reserved.
Lösungsorientiertes Team-Coaching by Jörg Middendorf and Ben Furman, Copyright © Springer Fachmedien Wiesbaden GmbH, ein Teil von Springer Nature 2019. All Rights Reserved.

ISSN 2731-4758　　　　　　　　ISSN 2731-4766　(electronic)
Business Guides on the Go
ISBN 978-3-031-07699-2　　　　ISBN 978-3-031-07700-5　(eBook)
https://doi.org/10.1007/978-3-031-07700-5

© The Editor(s) (if applicable) and The Author(s), under exclusive licence to Springer Nature Switzerland AG 2022
This work is subject to copyright. All rights are solely and exclusively licensed by the Publisher, whether the whole or part of the material is concerned, specifically the rights of reprinting, reuse of illustrations, recitation, broadcasting, reproduction on microfilms or in any other physical way, and transmission or information storage and retrieval, electronic adaptation, computer software, or by similar or dissimilar methodology now known or hereafter developed.
The use of general descriptive names, registered names, trademarks, service marks, etc. in this publication does not imply, even in the absence of a specific statement, that such names are exempt from the relevant protective laws and regulations and therefore free for general use.
The publisher, the authors, and the editors are safe to assume that the advice and information in this book are believed to be true and accurate at the date of publication. Neither the publisher nor the authors or the editors give a warranty, expressed or implied, with respect to the material contained herein or for any errors or omissions that may have been made. The publisher remains neutral with regard to jurisdictional claims in published maps and institutional affiliations.

This Springer imprint is published by the registered company Springer Nature Switzerland AG.
The registered company address is: Gewerbestrasse 11, 6330 Cham, Switzerland

Foreword

It was originally an innovative approach to psychotherapy. An approach that was very different from what mainstream psychotherapy was like at the time the approach was developed. When I specialized as a young medical doctor in psychiatry in the early 80s, psychotherapy was a popular method that everyone in the field of mental health wanted to learn. But what we learned in those days was very different from the solution-focused approach that this book is about. We learned that to help our patients overcome their psychological problems, we should ask them to visit us regularly for several years to talk about their life, their past, their childhood, their dreams… Psychotherapy meant figuring out how clients were haunted by their past.

But in the midst of this ethos, there were some interesting new trends burgeoning. One of these was called "brief therapy." It emerged in Palo Alto, California, where a group of researchers was trying to develop an innovative therapy method based on the uncommon therapy of Milton Erickson.

Erickson was a psychiatrist who specialized in hypnosis and whose ideas were at odds with mainstream psychiatry. Like Freud, he too spoke about the unconscious mind, but for him, the unconscious mind was not a warehouse of subconscious conflicts and repressed traumatic memories. On the contrary, he spoke about the unconscious mind as a rich source of resources, ideas, solutions, and learning experiences.

I became fascinated by Milton Erickson and the ideas presented by the Palo Alto brief therapy project. I had learned in my psychiatric studies to think that behind the problem that the client presents there is another problem, a more severe problem that needs to be uncovered and revealed. According to this logic, the client's problem is not their real problem; the real problem is an underlying problem that needs to be disclosed and treated. This psychotherapeutic canon was challenged by the burgeoning brief therapy movement, where it was replaced with a different and novel logic: the client's problem is not the real problem (the first part of the dictum is identical with the traditional dictum); the real problem is the way in which the client is trying to solve their problem. In brief therapy, the therapist does not try to shine the light on any hypothetical underlying problems, but instead on attempted solutions. "What have you tried to do to solve the problem? Has it worked? Would you be willing to try something different?" Brief therapists were not analysts or archaeologists. They were American pragmatists. "If it doesn't work, try something different" was one of their mottos.

The ideas of brief therapy were not chiseled into stone. They kept evolving. They spread to other areas in the work with people. There were many small teams of excited therapists around the world who investigated the idea and developed their own special modifications. One of these teams, headed by Steve De Shazer and Insoo Kim Berg, operated in Milwaukee. This team managed to develop a modification of brief therapy that was slightly different from what had been proposed by the team in Palo Alto. Their solution-focused brief therapy approach concentrates on the client's preferred future, on the client's own hopes and dreams. It is assumed that the client has all the resources and skills that they need to improve the quality of their life. So, what is then the role of the therapist or coach? What does he or she do to help the client achieve their goals? Therapists and coaches are hosts of meetings and the host is granted the authority to steer the conversation. The steering wheel for doing this is questions. By presenting solution-focused questions coaches can support their clients to make small changes that can lead to big differences in the future. In the first part of the book, you will become familiar with the rich variety of useful questions that the solution-focused therapists in Milwaukee and their successors developed over time. At the same time,

you will be given a simple and clear structure for a professional one-on-one coaching. Once you have covered part one, you will be rewarded with part two, where Jörg Middendorf takes you by the hand and exposes you to yet another development in the field of solution-focused work with individuals and teams that is known as Reteaming. Yes, you got it. Reteaming is just another
modification of the solution-focused approach composed of 12 steps—or actually 12 questions to be more precise. The approach was designed by Tapani Ahola and me in the 90s and it is founded on the principles of solution-focused brief therapy. It is, in fact, simply a modification of that approach, constructed for the purpose of introducing the solution-focused coaching into the realm of organizations, teams and groups.

You are in good hands. Jörg Middendorf is an experienced Reteaming coach. He has used this approach with clients for many years and is today an acclaimed and certified reteaming coach trainer. The book provides a delightful peek at the elegant—or magical—way in which he presents useful questions to his clients and builds them up to help them to talk differently, to think differently and to discover their own solutions.

Helsinki, Finland   Ben Furman

Acknowledgments

Part One was originally published in German with the title: Lösungsorientiertes Coaching by Jörg Middendorf, Copyright © Springer Fachmedien Wiesbaden GmbH, part of Springer Nature 2018, 2019. All rights reserved.

Part Two was originally published in German with the title: Lösungsorientiertes Team-Coaching by Jörg Middendorf and Ben Furman Copyright © Springer Fachmedien Wiesbaden GmbH, part of Springer Nature 2019. All rights reserved.

Special thanks to Jörg Schmidt! The visualizations for the book were created by Jörg Schmidt, who is a specialist for visualizations in trainings and workshops, based in Germany. All rights reserved.

einfach-visualisieren.com
Special thanks are due to Paul Williams for proofreading and his invaluable contribution to the translation from German into English. Paul Williams is a business coach and co-author of the book "The Illusion of Invincibility". inca-inc.com/en/

Praise for *Solution-focused Business Coaching*

"An extremely useful, practical and well-structured book for professional coaches and for those in a leadership role looking for inspiration and new approaches in managing people. Highly recommended!"
—Paul Williams and Andreas Krebs, *bestselling authors of The Illusion of Invincibility*

"The book provides a delightful peek at the elegant—or magical—way in which Jörg Middendorf presents useful questions to his clients and builds them up to help them to talk differently, to think differently and to discover their own solutions."
—Ben Furman, *Helsinki Brief Therapy Institute Ltd.*

Contents

Part I Individual Coaching — 1

1 It Is Not About Solutions! — 3
  1.1 An Initial Guide — 3
  1.2 Misunderstanding: The Solution-Focused Approach Focuses on Solutions — 5
  1.3 Misunderstanding: Problems Are Never Talked About in the SFC — 7
  1.4 Misunderstanding: Solution-Focused = Miracle Question!? — 8
  1.5 Conclusion — 8

2 If It's Not Broken, Don't Fix it — 11
  2.1 Basic Assumptions of the Solution-Focused Approach — 11
  2.2 The Classic Session of SFBT — 20

3 It Is Simple and Sometimes Easy — 23
  3.1 The Solution-Focused Coaching (SFC) Process — 23
  3.2 Define and Differentiate the Outcome — 28
      Transcript of a Real-Life Example — 31
      Fifty Questions Around Goals and the Preferred Future — 34

3.3	Recognize and Develop Resources	36
	Transcript of Real-Life Example: Continuation	40
	Fifty Questions to Recognize and Develop Resources	42
3.4	Recognize and Reinforce Progress	44
	Almost 50 Questions Around Progress	47
3.5	Adjourning	49
3.6	Mastering Challenging Situations	52

4 It Is More than a Miracle — 59
- 4.1 The Miracle Question and Its Children — 59
- 4.2 Scale Questions — 62
- 4.3 Formula First Session Task and Compliments — 67
- 4.4 Attentional Focus — 69

Part II Team Coaching: Reteaming* — 73

5 It Is All About Motivation: Reteaming* — 75
- 5.1 The Idea of Reteaming* — 75
- 5.2 The Five Factors of Motivation — 77

6 It Starts with a Motto: The Assignment — 83
- 6.1 The First Contact — 83
- 6.2 The Personal First Contact — 87

7 It Is About the Team's Future: The Team Coaching Workshop — 91
- 7.1 Joining — 91
- 7.2 Start Checklist: Flip Charts and Material to Start With — 98

8 It Is Only 12 Steps: The Team Coaching Workshop — 99
- 8.1 Our Future Dream — 99
- 8.2 Our Goal — 107
- 8.3 Our Supporters — 110
- 8.4 Our Benefit — 112

8.5	Our Progress So Far	113
8.6	Our Future Progress	115
8.7	Our Challenges	117
8.8	Our Confidence	118
8.9	Our Promise	119
8.10	Our Progress Monitoring	121
8.11	Our Strategies Against Setbacks	122
8.12	Our Celebration of Successes	124

Literature 127

Introduction

It Is Just an Innocent Question!

"What brings you to me?" As innocent as this question may sound, the consequences for the further course of the conversation can be profound. Steve de Shazer (co-founder of the solution-focused approach) experienced this first-hand when he worked with a family and asked this question. He only wanted to hear about the precise concern for which the family had come to him and his colleagues for counseling. The result, however, was a heated conversation between the family members and, at the end of a turbulent counseling session, 27 different problems named by the family as the reason for the counseling! The counseling team, led by de Shazer, found it difficult to come up with an intervention that could address these 27 problems at the end of the session. So they asked the family to simply pay attention over the next two weeks to what was going well in their lives and what should be maintained. After two weeks, the family members came into counseling and reported that everything was going much better now and that they felt their problems were solved. Solution Focusing was born!—Or at the very least, it was certainly one of the key starting points…

It was similarly enlightening for me when, towards the end of my psychology studies in the 90s, I got a new professor in clinical psychology (Prof. Dr. Schiepek) who told us for the first time about systemic approaches and Steve de Shazer's solution-focused approach. Until then, in clinical psychology, I had mainly dealt with the diagnosis and analysis of problems, problematic behaviors and the environment in which the problematic behavior took place. Now, suddenly, I heard that the path to greater satisfaction may not have been about understanding the problems at all, but about having an attractive goal and recognizing one's own resources. The solution may actually be completely independent of the problems! Fascinated by the ease of this approach, we immediately tried out this new way of thinking on ourselves, invited test clients to work with us and even received a visit from Steve de Shazer to experience his work live. It quickly became clear that solution-focused work not only opened new possibilities in therapy and counseling, but also opened completely new perspectives on every form of human interaction. This was the beginning of a now more than 20-year-long enthusiasm for the solution-focused approach and a relative lack of interest in problems and root cause analysis.

Since the beginnings of the solution-focused (SF) approach, it has been constantly developed further, so that there is now a worldwide community practicing the principles of the approach in the field of therapy, social work, coaching, work with schools, teams, and entire organizations. Therefore, in the following, we will not only discuss the SF approach according to de Shazer et al, but also take a closer look at the SF approach in working with teams, called Reteaming®, according to Ben Furman and Tapani Ahola. Since I got to know the Reteaming® approach in 2008, there is no other way of working with teams for me, because success is practically guaranteed! Reteaming® has the same intuitive ease and pragmatism about it as the approach by de Shazer and has, in addition, helpful steps to deal with critical team-dynamics.

With this book, I would now like to pass on some of the enthusiasm and pragmatism of solution focusing. It is primarily aimed at coaches and consultants who would like to enrich their work by the solution-focused approach. At the same time, the basic principles of the approach can be transferred to all forms of professional work with people. SF is not meant to be a new dogma, but an alternative way that is well tested, works extremely well and, above all, is fun to use. Enjoy reading!

Jörg Middendorf

Part I

Individual Coaching

1

It Is Not About Solutions!

1.1 An Initial Guide

It was not until 1985 that Solution-Focused Brief Therapy (SFBT) was presented in a comprehensive form to the general public in a book ("Keys to solution in brief therapy") by Steve de Shazer. Steve de Shazer, Insoo Kim Berg et al. had already intensively studied new forms of intervention and their effectiveness in psychotherapy at the end of the 1970s. They were also influenced by the work of Milton Erickson and his hypnotherapeutic approach. His understanding of the client's resources as a starting point for solving problems and living a more satisfying life were an important starting point for the basic principles of SFBT.

De Shazer was also strongly influenced by the work of the Palo Alto group (MRI, Mental Research Institute) and the Milan School of Family Therapists (Centro per lo Studio della Famiglia). Both groups developed brief therapeutic approaches as part of their family therapy concept. The exploration of these systemic brief therapeutic approaches, together with the resource-oriented view of Milton Erickson, formed the fertile ground for further development, which then resulted in the establishment of the Brief Family Therapy Center (BFTC), founded in 1978 by Steve de Shazer, Insoo Kim Berg, and others.

The goal of BFTC was to find the most effective and efficient ways to help clients. In the process, a realization very soon emerged that set the BFTC approach apart from all established therapeutic approaches: interventions that lead to resolution need have nothing to do with the root causes of client's problems. Problems can be complicated and multi-faceted, they can have a long history, and they can be serious. However, all this does not mean that the interventions leading to the solution must also be complicated or multi-layered.

Steve de Shazer used the image of a lock pick to explain this. In this picture, the problem is a complicated lock which the clients cannot open with the means at their disposal. The solution, however, is not hidden in the lock (problem), but in the use of the appropriate key. To open the complicated lock, it is not necessary to have an equally complicated key, but a simple lock pick that can open this lock is sufficient. It is precisely this abandonment of problem analysis that distinguishes the SF approach from almost all other therapy and coaching approaches, which assume that problem analysis is an important and indispensable part of change work. This view is also consistent with the social constructivist foundation of BFTC's work: we create our own social reality upon which we act and react. When clients describe their reality, including their problem, it is highly unlikely that I really understand and see things exactly as clients meant them. After all, the concepts and interrelationships we accept as real, do not necessarily apply in the world of our clients and vice versa. However, it is also not necessary to fully understand our clients and their reality, as my understanding of their situation does not bring clients any closer to their solution. Rather, it is important that, following an intervention, our clients do something different in their world, thus setting in motion a process and momentum that brings them closer to their individual solution. According to de Shazer, therefore, there is no such thing as genuine understanding between client and therapist, so there is therefore no point in analyzing the client's problem. Useful forms of misunderstanding are quite sufficient. The solution-focused approach assumes that the preferred future can and must be constructed and created only by our clients. We are not slaves to our past, but can design our own future, and then independently define our own steps to arrive at that future. The therapist and counselor help to discover the desirable future as well as the client's own resources so that the goal can become a reality.

All clients find the necessary resources within them and their environment. Therefore, small changes are often enough to set a larger change in motion on the desired path.

Since the first formulation of these basic ideas and principles, the approach has been further sharpened. At the same time, many ideas of the SF approach have also been adopted—or at least adopted partly—by other approaches to counseling, so that misunderstandings about the original SF approach keep arising. Some are rooted in the early days of the approach, and some have arisen from the adoption and modification of SF methods by other approaches. The following misunderstandings and their remedies will help to provide a better orientation about what constitutes the SF approach.

1.2 Misunderstanding: The Solution-Focused Approach Focuses on Solutions

This is exactly what the SF approach does not do, since a solution is always a solution to a problem. However, as we have already seen, SF Coaching (SFC) is not interested in problems. The client is not even asked "What brings you to me?" or "What is your concern?" at the beginning of coaching, because this automatically encourages clients to describe their problem—as they have probably done many times to friends or colleagues. In the SF approach, this is considered to be neither goal-oriented nor helpful—but above all, it is simply seen as unnecessary.

The first question in SFC today is often: "What are your best hopes from our talking today?" (introduced by BRIEF London). This means that the client's preferred future is established directly. The SF approach takes the desired future as the starting point for further coaching. If this future is achieved, then dealing with the problem has essentially taken care of itself. After all, in the preferred future, the problem no longer exists, otherwise it would not be the preferred future. Instead of the problem, there is now something else. And this "other thing" is described as part of the desired future. So, to solve a problem, I do not necessarily have to focus on the problem. It is sufficient to approach my preferred future step by step.

In conclusion, SF does not mean supporting clients in finding solutions to their problems in a resource-oriented way, but is all about helping them to develop a detailed picture of their preferred future. By describing this future precisely—"painting the picture"—clients increase the likelihood of achieving it. For coaching, this means that the coach supports clients in the conversation to become aware of their possibilities, because often clients are cut off from their own resources by their view of the problem and are not able to recognize what competencies they actually have available.

According to SF, the past does not dictate what the client's future should look like. According to this view, clients find helpful impulses for their own development in the clearest possible description of their own future, which is understood as something created and negotiable. This radical kind of future orientation is also something that distinguishes the SF approach from many other coaching approaches.

Other approaches often place a stronger emphasis on the past, such as psychodynamic approaches, or the influences of current contextual variables of the clients, such as the systemic approaches.

However, why is the approach called "Solution Focused?" There are historical reasons for this: The group of researchers in Palo Alto around John Weakland, Richard Fisch, Paul Watzlawick, etc. published an article in 1974 entitled "Brief Therapy: Focused Problem Resolution." In 1986, Steve de Shazer, Insoo Kim Berg, Eve Lipchick et al. wrote another article that referred to the Weakland et al. article. The title of the de Shazer et al. article "Brief Therapy: Focused Solution Development" was intended to make it clear that there were some similarities in the approaches, but also significant differences: Thus, the name Solution Focused was established. Nevertheless, from today's perspective, Preferred Future Approach or Future Focused Approach would have been a more appropriate name for it. Equally, for coaching, the most appropriate name would be Preferred Future Coaching or Future Focused Coaching. However, to avoid having two names for the same approach, we will stick with the traditional Solution-Focused Coaching (SFC).

1.3 Misunderstanding: Problems Are Never Talked About in the SFC

The focus on the preferred future does not mean that problems cannot be discussed in SFC. The degree of suffering for many clients is often too great for the problem to be ignored. In fact, it is often important that the level of suffering and current coping strategies are explicitly acknowledged by the coach. However, this does not mean that the coach necessarily has to ask about or specifically try and understand the problem.

We are susceptible and, indeed, may have been trained to see the world from a bio-mechanistic or cybernetic point of view, with the tendency to look for a mono-causal or multi-causal hypothesis for the reasons behind the problems our clients are facing. In the case of engines, be they simple or complex, this makes sense. After all, if an engine is broken, I need to find out what the cause of the problem is so that the engine can then be fixed. But people function differently than machines and exploring the problem and its causes is not necessary. Nevertheless, this bio-mechanistic approach is often transferred to work with people.

When regularly using SFC, it becomes apparent time and again that the desired future has little to do with the problem that was the reason for the visit to the coach. Thus, the actual problem (e.g., "a disruptive employee") often recedes into the background and the focus turns to the client's goal (e.g., "to be a successful leader").

Problems thus play a role in SFC regarding the reason for the coaching or the appreciation of the suffering and the client's handling of the situation, but for the outcome of the coaching, they play only a minor role. As a consequence, and from a broader perspective, organizations should not view coaching as a general repair service for the problems of managers and employees. Coaching should be seen as specific form of human resources activity that supports the self-determined development of people. And it does not need a problem to do that!

1.4 Misunderstanding: Solution-Focused = Miracle Question!?

This absolute focus on the future has developed and evolved within the SF approach over a number of years. For example, most coaches are familiar with the "Miracle Question," the second major export hit of the SF approach, alongside the so-called scale questions. The miracle question has served so well that for a while, it was used as a fixed standard in every SF conversation. However, the miracle question needs a problem for it to work. This limits the effectiveness of this question to the area of the specific problem. Over time, this has led to it being used less frequently by SF coaches today. It has been overtaken by the so-called "best hope" question referred to earlier, which focuses on the desired future. The SF approach of 1987 is not the SF approach of 2022, even if the basic assumptions remain the same.

1.5 Conclusion

Several consequences for the work with people arise from the above. These consequences should serve the reader as an orientation when we look more concretely at the methods of SF Coaching:

Coaching Clients …

- … do not need a doctor to make a diagnosis.
  - Solution-Focused Coaching is fundamentally different from other forms of coaching, as it does away with any diagnosis and analysis.

- ... only need a lock pick to open the lock.
  - Concrete ways to increase satisfaction and achieve goals are independent of possible problems.
- ... are the experts for their lives!
  - We shape our own future—We are all experts about what constitutes our own well-being.
- ... find their own way!
  - The coach supports the coaching clients in finding the appropriate path to a self-designed future—but does not prescribe the path.
- ... already have everything that is necessary!
  - Coaching clients have all the resources they need to make their lives better.
- ... change in any case!
  - Change cannot be prevented—Solution-Focused Coaching helps clients take the direction of change that is right for them.
- ... do not need a narcissist as a coach!
  - Coaching clients are always more knowledgeable about their own lives than the consultant. Coaching is not about showing how brilliant I am as a coach, but about creating a framework in which clients can use their own brilliance in the sense of their preferred future.

2

If It's Not Broken, Don't Fix it

2.1 Basic Assumptions of the Solution-Focused Approach

Solution-Focused Brief Therapy (SFBT) is not an approach that has mainly developed based on theoretical considerations. Rather, it emerged from experience in daily practice and has evolved through constant engagement with clients, therapists, and other counselors. Of course, these counselors shared similar basic assumptions, but there was no theoretical, self-contained overall concept that preceded the interventions and processes of the solution-focused approach. If anything, a mutually understood and accepted foundation emerged and evolved over a number of years, describing a practice that had been in place for a longer time. Therefore, in the various writings of de Shazer and his colleagues, one will always find different aspects described as basic assumptions of the approach. These aspects can range from philosophical aspects from Ludwig Wittgenstein through basic assumptions taken from related counseling approaches (e.g., the MRI in Palo Alto or Milton Erickson), to very concrete guiding ideas of solution-focused work, which are presented below.

In a handout for students, Insoo Kim Berg very pertinently described two central premises of the SF approach as follows:

> ... the future is created and negotiated, and is not a slave to the past events in a person's life ...
> ... the client has all the resources, skills, and knowledge to make their life better, if they decide that this is good for them and that they want things to be better for themselves.

These two assumptions are based on a set of systemic views about the nature of problems, solutions, clients and consultants. For example, most problems arise from the client's perspective (social construction) and their interaction with the world (contextuality). By believing that one is doing "the right thing" repeatedly, problems are often perpetuated in the first place. Solutions, on the other hand, emerge when one does something differently than before.

Emphasis on the social context is also of particular importance for the solution: changes in one element of the system or the relationship of the elements to each other, always affect the other elements of the system. A system here can be both a social system (team, group, families, ...) or the inner-psychological system of a person. This also means that changes cannot be prevented as soon as even a small part of the system starts to move. To make progress towards a solution, it is therefore often sufficient that "small things" change. This principle is independent of the size or complexity of the original problem, because solutions work independently of the problem. In my view, the clearest summary of the basic assumptions of solution-focused work can be found in Steve de Shazer's last book, published posthumously ("More Than Miracles," Steve de Shazer and Yvonne Dolan, 2007). Eight major tenets of SFBT are summarized there.

1. "If It Isn't Broken, Don't Fix It"

This tenet sounds almost banal, but it is of crucial importance because it emphasizes the client's competence. Once clients have found a way to deal with the problem, it is not up to the consultant to find a problem behind the problem or to discover or invent hidden, unconscious problems. There is also no goal behind the goal, that the consultant must find out, or define an even "better" goal (at least from the consultant's point of view). There is also no compulsion to grow, just because a psychological school of thought sees such so-called growth as a fundamental part of human fulfillment. Especially in coaching, we have to say goodbye to the idea that we are facing a person with some kind of deficit who, therefore, has to be helped. In coaching, two competent adults meet at eye level to address the client's desired future and their resources for achieving it. Thus, clients do not need to be "fixed" (cured, taught, improved, …) in any way. Thinking aloud and looking at a situation together is only meant to broaden the perspective, so that currently inaccessible possibilities come back into the coaching client's field of vision.

2. "If It Works, Do More of It"

This principle also starts with the client's own intrinsic competence. If clients have already shown behaviors that have led to an improvement of the situation, it is important to reinforce them, since they obviously work for them. Importantly, the consultant does not judge whether this is a good or bad strategy to deal with the situation, but helps clients to discover resources in their own behaviors that are already there and that can be used more effectively or more often, if necessary. In SFC this is done by focusing attention on what works. Many coaching clients are so cut off from their resources by the pressure caused by the current problem that they are not able to recognize what is actually already working and what competencies they have available. The coaching can already be successfully concluded at this point, by virtue of the fact that clients are able to regain access to all the behaviors and strategies that already work.

3. "If It's Not Working, Do Something Different"

This insight was described a long time ago by Paul Watzlawick when he noted that most problems first arise because the same approaches to solving them are always pursued. If these attempts at a solution don't lead to the desired success, no matter how brilliant or logical they may seem, it is better to try something else. This is true for both the client and the coach. If the coach uses interventions that are not taken up by the client, then it is not a matter of insisting on something, but simply of doing something else as a coach.

4. "Small Steps Can Lead to Big Changes"

Here it is emphasized that the solution-focused approach concentrates on many small but feasible steps rather than on the big change. This tenet also emphasizes the systemic view that movement in one part of the system always results in movement of the entire system. Especially in coaching, this tenet is of special importance, since here we usually work with adult, competent personalities who have a multitude of resources and behavioral strategies at their disposal. Once they are in motion, our clients can often very quickly take the next helpful steps without the support of the coach.

5. "The Solution Is Not Necessarily Directly Related to the Problem"

Instead of starting with a diagnosis and problem analysis to arrive at the appropriate intervention that will hopefully lead to the goal, the solution-focused approach takes the opposite approach. We start with the preferred future and then look for resources that will bring us closer to that future. The difference is striking! Dealing with a preferred future usually releases creativity and other positive resources. In contrast, dealing with the problem rarely leads to euphoria and joy. This becomes especially clear when working with groups: If one begins by analyzing a team's problem, one will quickly notice how much the group retreats and builds up lines of defense, since everyone instinctively realizes that they may come out as the guilty party in the root cause analysis. If, on the other hand, one directly assumes a positive future, the question of cause or blame does not even arise. After all, it is only about achieving something positive and seeing who can make what contribution. A completely different atmosphere for working is created. And this is also true in individual coaching. A positive image of the future as a starting point releases the client's resources, which can then lead to solutions that one would not have come up with if the starting point had been the problem.

For SFC today, one could take this tenet even further and say: *The preferred future is not related to the problem.*

6. "The Language for Solution Development Is Different from that Needed to Describe a Problem"

Of all the tenets, this is probably the one that relates most directly to the analytic philosophy of Ludwig Wittgenstein. It draws attention to the fact that talking about problems makes a different view of the situation likely than when talking about solutions. (See also the comments on the fifth tenet). Conscious use of language is therefore a core competency of solution-focused coaches. This requires a sharp rethinking of some of the implicit assumptions one had of one's own language and its potential impact on the other person. Problematical language would include questions such as "What is the problem? Why is it so difficult? How does it make you feel when it doesn't work?" etc. Solution language, on the other hand, asks "What is your best hope from our conversation? Where are the first signs of this preferred future? How did you manage to get this far?" etc.

7. "No Problems Happen All the Time; There Are Always Exceptions that Can Be Utilized"

Change cannot be prevented in the real world. There is no such thing as perfect standstill. Therefore, the precise nature of a problem cannot always be static and one hundred percent the same all the time. This is used traditionally in solution-focused work as a starting point for one of the key interventions: When was the problem less bad? When was the situation better? This difference between when the problem was strong and when it was less strong can be used in conjunction with the ideas of tenets number 2 and 4: Do more of whatever it was you did that caused the problem to be less severe! No matter how small the step, it is a step towards a solution. In recent years, it has widely become accepted in parts of the solution-focused community not to even look for "exceptions to the problem" anymore, because this would bring the problem back into focus. Instead, one tries to discover together with the clients consistently first "signs for the preferred future". This is a further development that is certainly in the spirit of Steve and Insoo, since the focus is now even more focused on the future.

For the SFC today, this tenet could consequently be reformulated as follows: *There are always signs of the preferred future.*

8. "The Future Is Both Created and Negotiable"

This tenet we have already seen above in the two premises handed-out to students by Insoo Kim Berg. SFC sees clients as the master of their own future. Perhaps clients need a little support in recognizing their possibilities, but there is no compulsion from the past that dictates what the future should look like. Again, it is clear how little analyzing the past and understanding the problem can help us in creating the preferred future.

These tenets clarify central assumptions and principles of solution-focused work with clients. In fact, it is irrelevant whether clients are worked with in the therapeutic field, in coaching or in social work. The above principles can be applied to work with all people. It should be clear from what has been said so far that these tenets are supposed to be helpful assumptions rather than rigid dogmas. After all, there is no such thing as complete standstill and solution-focused work is constantly evolving as well as everything else.

For coaching, one might think that nowadays many of the basic assumptions mentioned are almost common sense. Nevertheless, even in coaching, there is often still talk of a diagnostic phase, problem analyses and goals behind the goal. This shows that a traditional problem-oriented attitude is hidden sometimes behind a superficial solution-and resource-orientation. This attitude will inevitably be reflected in language and prevent a consistent use of solution-focused language (see sixth tenet) from doing its work. This is, of course, perfectly legitimate if it is done consciously and is intentional on the part of the consultant. If, on the other hand, one genuinely wants to work in a solution-focused way, it is worthwhile reflecting on one's own practice, based on the tenets, and systematically checking implicit presuppositions in coaching to date, in order to systematically strengthen the already existing solution-focused elements of one's own work.

2.2 The Classic Session of SFBT

In principle, in SF approaches, every conversation should be conducted as if it were also the last conversation with that person. Since it is assumed that even small changes are sufficient to make a decisive difference, there is no reason to assume that solution-focused counseling (coaching or even therapy) should or even must take place over a number of sessions. The following section describes a classical process of solution-focused conversation. Depending on the source and the time of publication, even the classic flow may show differences, as the approach has constantly evolved.

1. Joining
As with any form of counseling, there is a joining phase in SFBT, in which a positive working atmosphere should be created. Here, if possible, the topic or the problem is not yet discussed at length, but only the

framework and the agreements that are important for the coaching and the trustful cooperation. The goal is to build a positive and trusting working atmosphere. Nevertheless, describing the problem is a primary and urgent concern for many clients, which is why Insoo Kim Berg and Peter De Jong also speak of the fact that the first step can also be or often is the description of the problem (1998).

2. Goal
At this point, in most other approaches, there would be an anamnesis, diagnosis, or problem analysis. SFBT rejects this as unhelpful and instead explores the client's goal. True to the basic assumption that the goal is independent of the problem anyway, but in the end, it is all about achieving the goal, from now on one only talks about the goal.

3. Exceptions to the Problem
The SFBT practitioner now helps clients by asking questions to find exceptions to the current problem situation that are already moving a little towards achieving the goal. These exceptions are further explored to facilitate the client's access to their current resources that may bring them or have already brought them closer to the goal.

4. Scaling
With these resources and exceptions in mind, the clients are now asked to indicate where they stand today on a scale of 0–10 (10 = complete goal achievement). The work with scales is described in more detail in Sects. 3.3 and 4.2. Here it is sufficient to point out that the scale makes it possible to describe differences, to divide the goal into smaller units and to help reveal further resources (How did you make it to scale level X?). Then the behavior is described that the clients will show to enable them to take the next step on the scale and move further towards achieving the goal. This automatically means that the clients themself describe both the direction and the possible content of the change.

5. Compliments, Task, and Conclusion

The clients now have an idea of how to proceed and take responsibility for doing so if they judge, it will be helpful to them. In classical SFBT, a short break was inserted before the end of the session, during which the therapist withdrew and reflected once again on what the clients had achieved so far and what tasks would support further progress after the counseling session. After the break, the therapist first gave compliments about the client's skills and the successes already achieved. Afterwards, the therapist suggested a homework task, that is, a task in the sense of a behavioral experiment that would support the clients in having new experiences, seeing positive aspects in their life, and getting a little closer to their goal. Whether there should be another session at all, in which, for example, the results of the behavioral experiment could be discussed, was discussed at the end of the session, or simply left to the clients, who could turn to the counselor again if necessary.

Since the earliest days of Solution-Focused Brief Therapy, the approach has naturally evolved and been adapted for a variety of settings. These developments have been driven by both De Shazer and Insoo Kim Berg, the Brief Family Therapy Center (or the Solution-Focused Brief Therapy Association), and thousands of solution-focused practitioners around the world. Therefore, the description of the classic session does not serve to describe the only useful approach, but rather should be understood as a starting point for the further description of solution-focused coaching.

3

It Is Simple and Sometimes Easy

3.1 The Solution-Focused Coaching (SFC) Process

> This section describes the beginning of solution-focused coaching and the importance of relationship building. The aim of this phase is to provide clients with a transparent overview of the coaching, the terms of the contract, get to know the coach, and understand the coaching approach. At the same time, an initial insight into some of the resources of the clients can be gained. The following methods and strategies are discussed in this section:
>
> - Joining
> - Resource-oriented client introduction
> - Dealing with problem talk

Context and Joining

SFC has three core phases:

1. Define and differentiate outcomes
2. Recognize and develop resources
3. Recognize and reinforce progress

These core phases are framed by joining (establishing contact) at the beginning of the process and adjourning (concluding for the moment) at the end of the specific session. In the following section, the joining is described, which defines the framework and the working alliance between coach and client and is therefore of great importance in practice.

Many empirical data suggest that the effectiveness of coaching depends less on a specific method than on the relationship between coach and client. Therefore, it is also important for SFC to build this relationship at the beginning of a conversation. In this first phase of coaching, a kind of working alliance (= joining) should therefore be established between coach and client. The goal of this alliance is to achieve an improvement of the situation in the client's interest. For this alliance to be established, it is helpful that clients …

- … know who their discussion partner is.
- … are aware of the contractual framework and conditions.
- … are positive that they will be treated respectfully and that the discussion is confidential.
- … develop an idea of how client and coach will work together.

We will not go into the contractual regulations in detail, since solution-focused coaching is of course no different from other forms of coaching in this respect. Nevertheless, I would like to emphasize that it is important that there is complete transparency about all contractual aspects so that clients know exactly what they are getting into. Components of a coaching agreement are therefore at least:

- Designation of the contracting parties (client, coach, contracting partner)
- Planned scope of the coaching
- Fee agreement as well as possible additional costs (e.g., travel expenses)
- Location of coaching (e.g., coach's office)
- Cancellation policies (e.g., what amount of notice is required to cancel a coaching session without incurring charges)
- Rules on confidentiality

In addition, it may be useful to contractually stipulate or explicitly discuss further conditions. These include details of invoicing, aspects of quality assurance (evaluation), agreed interim review meetings and final meetings (e.g., if in an organizational context the client is not identical with the contract partner), involvement of third parties (e.g., as feedback providers), liability issues or reference to ethical guidelines to which the coach subscribes and binds themself (e.g., through membership of a professional association such as the International Coaching Federation—ICF). Particularly in business coaching, a high-quality coaching agreement will help prevent any confusion, lack of clarity or confidentiality issues between the coach, the client and the contracting partner, which might harm the trustful relationship between these parties.

Of particular importance in SFC is the scope of the coaching, as the coaching process can be completed after only one session. In SFC every session is treated as the last one. As a coach, we don't measure our success based on running-up as many coaching hours as possible with our clients. Our business is based on achieving as many satisfied clients as possible. Therefore, it is important that the coach is first and foremost aware of how to structure the first session: As a non-binding get-to-know-you-meeting, as is often expected in companies, or as the first regular coaching session, which of course must also be billed. We will return to this question a little later, when we have discussed the relationship part of joining.

In addition to contractual issues, relationship building is of central importance in joining. Without a positive relationship, there will be no (successful) coaching. With this in mind, it is important not to slip accidentally into problem analysis by asking a thoughtless question at the beginning of the contact with clients, such as "What is the problem?". This would lead the conversation directly to the typical problem talk. In SFC we avoid any kind of problem analysis because it does not activate the client's resources, which are so important for helping clients towards improving the situation. That is why the frequently used questions "What brings you to me?" or "What is your concern?" are also not recommended. The best approach is to proceed as you would with almost any such conversation with a stranger, and begin with a brief personal introduction. Usually, the coach starts by introducing themself briefly by telling something about their work as a coach and some other aspects of their life in general. One introduces oneself as both a professional and a private person, which helps most clients to establish emotional contact with the coach. A kick-off for the introduction of the client can look something like this:

> *"Now I would like to know a bit more about you. Who are you? What do you spend your time doing? And above all, what do you especially like doing and what do you do particularly well?"*

This kind of mutual introduction makes it clear from the start that the SFC values the preferences and strengths of clients. The focus on resources thus already begins with the introduction of the clients. In the clients' description about the things that they particularly like to do and that they are particularly good at, there are many resources hidden away that can be made use of later in the coaching. At the same time, one can already express appreciation about the strengths and abilities of the client. In so doing, one is creating a positive atmosphere with a compliment right at the very beginning of the coaching. This kind of communication additionally demonstrates the solution-focused approach and establishes a respectful and appreciative interaction, which should be the basis of further cooperation. In SFC clients are not put in the role of a deficit-ridden counterpart who must now be healed by the expert. Two people with different strengths meet at eye level to engage in a constructive and helpful conversation.

A short description of the nature of this particular coaching process naturally follows when you briefly go into why you have asked these questions:

> *"Thank you for your introduction and for the insight into what you do well and what you like to do! This helps me to get a first impression of you. In coaching, it is important to me that we reach your goals. For this purpose, I will ask questions that allow me to learn something about your competencies and resources. In doing so, we will draw on your strengths and resources so that we can do all we can to help ensure that you will reach your goal. I can't guarantee goal achievement, of course, but I will do my best to support you."*

Other questions in this phase can be general questions about the goal of the coaching. In most systemically oriented coaching approaches, questions such as:

> "What is the goal of our collaboration?"
> "How would you know whether the coaching has been successful for you?"
> "What will be different if the coaching has been successful?"
> "How will you know that we can finish the coaching?"

Even if you as a coach have not explicitly asked about the problem, it may well be that clients start to talk about "their problem" directly on their own initiative. SFC does not mean that you interrupt clients and stop them from doing this, as this would not be very respectful and appreciative. Therefore, clients are given the opportunity to talk about their problem if they start to do so on their own initiative. However, this so-called "problem talk" should not be encouraged by active listening or other signs of interest, such as follow-up questions. The coach listens to the problem talk as neutrally as possible and expresses their appreciation of the difficulty of the situation and the client's coping strategies. If this appreciation of the complexity or severity of the situation were to be missing, a break in the joining, the working alliance, could easily occur. So if clients enter into problem talk on their own initiative, the coach needs to strike a fine balance between accepting the need for clients to describe their problem, while ensuring a prompt but smooth switch to the so-called "solution talk," the actual core of SFC, which will be described in more detail below.

With the solution talk, we are already in the middle of the coaching process and could start working on the goal of the coaching. However, we have already mentioned above that it has become common practice (at least in Germany), especially in the context of organizations, for there to be an initial meeting free of charge, and only then does the client decide on one or the other coach, and only then is a contract concluded and the chargeable part of the coaching begins. Very often, clients are obliged by their organization to see at least two coaches before deciding which one to choose.

On the one hand, this makes little sense for solution-focused coaching, as this can end after just 1 hour. Even if the comparison is very lame, one would not expect a physician to not be paid for the first hour. At the same time, one can make a virtue out of the (questionable) custom and thus elegantly separate the getting to know each other and the problem talk from the actual coaching. Here, too, the problem talk is not encouraged or intensified. If it nevertheless takes place, one allows it, as described above, expresses one's appreciation and recognition and leaves it behind in the getting-to-know-you conversation. This allows the coach to begin coaching free of any problem talk by talking directly about the clients' preferred future. In addition, the focus of clients can already be directed to their resources by asking them to pay attention to everything that should not be changed, because it already works for the clients, until the next meeting (see also Sect. 4.3 Formula First Session Task). If it is organizationally possible to use the first meeting completely for coaching, the core phase of SFC, the solution talk, follows directly after the mutual introduction.

3.2 Define and Differentiate the Outcome

In this section you will learn how to design the first phase of the solution talk. The goal of this phase is to develop a clear description of a preferred future. The following methods and strategies are discussed in this section:

- Solution Talk
- The Miracle Question
- The "what else" joker and 6 seconds rule
- The Best Hope Question
- Questions about the goal in the "as-if" framework
- Differentiation of the preferred future

After the joining, we start directly with the detailed description of the desired outcome of the coaching, regardless of whether we are still in the first session or we have previously had a non-binding "get-to-know-you" meeting. The central topic at the beginning of the solution talk is: What if the problem no longer exists? How do things now look instead? The classic question of SFBT for this is the miracle question (see Sect. 4.1 for a detailed description):

> *"Imagine that after we finish our session today, you go home, do the things you usually do, have dinner, maybe watch a little TV, etc. and at some point you go to bed.*
> *While you are asleep, a miracle happens. The miracle is that the problem that you are here for today has been solved, just like that!*
> *How will you know the next morning that the miracle has happened?"*

Evan George, Chris Iveson and Harvey Ratner (BRIEF London) suggest an alternative to the miracle question by asking their clients right at the beginning of the session, "What are your best hopes from our work together?" The "Best Hope Question" is used more often today in business coaching, because here we do not need a problem to be solved—not even by a miracle. We can start right away with the preferred future of our clients. However, the goal of the miracle question and the best hope question is to get a detailed description of the desired future. How do clients notice that the problem no longer exists? What does their preferred future look like? In their behavior—in their daily experiences? How would other people in the client's environment notice it? The more clearly the clients describe what will be different, the clearer the goal of the coaching becomes. It is immensely useful in focusing on the helpful aspects of the client's behavior which is now different. In this way, you not only get a clear description of the preferred future of the clients, but also a description of the desired behavior and thus a clear description of the aspects that could or should change.

By the way, it makes an enormous difference whether you ask, "How would you behave?" or "What in your behavior do you notice that will be different after the miracle has happened?" The first question is difficult for many clients to answer. After all, if they already knew how they should behave differently, they probably wouldn't be taking part in a coaching! Interestingly, it is often easier to describe how you will notice a change, and thus arrive at the description of the desired behavior via a small detour. One creates an "as-if" frame by letting the reality be described after the change has occurred. So the question contains the request to pretend that the desired state is already reality and then to describe it. Since you are asked to describe a state and not to think about what to do next, answering questions in the as-if frame is much easier.

The fact that the miracle question is not just a question, but a dialog about the desired state, should already have become clear and will be explained in more detail later. It is important to mention here that one can be quite persistent in describing the miracle or the preferred future. Therefore, as a coach, you should not be sparing with the most important question of solution-focused conversation: "What else?" "What else?" is an extremely open question, into which no content can be smuggled by the coach (unlike e.g. "Have you thought about talking to each other …?") and which can have a strongly stimulating effect for clients. So if clients seem to be finished with the description of the new situation without any problem, the coach should wait at least 6 seconds and wait to hear if there isn't something else forthcoming. If this "pause" of 6 seconds is not enough to move the clients to further descriptions of the preferred future, the coach simply asks, "What else?" and waits again—at least 6 seconds. Usually, more valuable details about the hoped-for target state will then come. The waiting (6-second rule) and the question "What else?" can now happily be repeated three to five times before no more new information will come. Since this question is almost always useful and can hardly be applied too often, we also call it the "what else" joker.

Differentiate the Outcomes
Once the desired future has been described, it is a matter of differentiating this future to make it even more vivid and to check whether the desired state is as positive as was hoped. For this purpose, it is helpful to talk about the effects of achieving the goal.

> "What impact will this change in behavior have? What difference will it make? Who else will notice the difference?"

With these questions, we deepen the clarity about the preferred future and at the same time invite the clients to talk in more detail about consequences of the change. Sometimes at this point, the clients may also encounter undesirable consequences for themself and others in their environment. Then it is necessary to change the target picture in such a way that it really fits and that all possible consequences, as far as one can foresee them at all, are desirable. Here, too, one should not skimp on our "what else" joker and leave enough pauses so that the clients can answer thoughtfully.

Transcript of a Real-Life Example

COACH: Thank you so much for being here. I'm very glad you're here today.
CLIENT: Me too.
COACH: So without further ado, what is your best hope in terms of the impact of our conversation today on your everyday life?
CLIENT: (…) That's a good question. My best hope? I want to be more consistent in my goals and stick to things more. I want to have the motivation and some techniques to really change something.
COACH: Motivation to really change something—pursue goals more consistently.
CLIENT: Yes.
COACH: Okay. What else?
CLIENT: That I know how to do that. How to practically get rid of a pattern or a habit that I have, how to … how to get rid of that.
COACH: Okay. You want to have the motivation to change something and have an idea how to do it?
CLIENT: Yes.
COACH: Okay. What difference will that make if you have the motivation, and you have an idea of how to tackle this?
CLIENT: Many situations in my everyday life would be more relaxed.
COACH: Okay. They would be more relaxed. What does it look like when they are more relaxed?
CLIENT: Much less stress, I'm more relaxed, I have this (…) I'd have a completely different time management.
COACH: Okay. Different time management. What does it look like when you have different time management?
CLIENT: That would have a structure that I could get comfortable with. So I would actually have a structure in the first place that would cause me less stress.

COACH: Okay. How would you see that you have that structure?

CLIENT: I would notice it by not running out of time or being pressed for time.

COACH: What else?

CLIENT: Yes. I'd see that I simply did the right things at the right time, so I don't have to do something in a hurry, at the last minute, where I end up feeling like I didn't do it well.

COACH: And that's desirable for you?

CLIENT: That's very desirable for me to change that. Yes.

COACH: Okay. Let's just imagine something: Let's imagine overnight that would be the case. So you have the time management that you envision, the structure that you envision. That's all there. It miraculously happened overnight. You wake up in the morning, but since it happened overnight, you don't know about it yet. How would you notice that things are different?

CLIENT: I think I would know directly what my to-dos are for the day. And I'd immediately have the feeling that this is doable, I can already get this done on this day, in the time that I have set for myself. So that I can go to training that evening completely relaxed, without having to count the minutes, without somehow having the stress that I'm too late or I have to skip something, or I even that I can't do it.

COACH: What else?

CLIENT: I think I'd do it pretty quickly ... Exactly. The ideal state would be, I know everything I'm going to do today, I'm going to get make a good start to the day and stay well on schedule.

COACH: Okay. So that would be the feeling you would get—already in the morning.

CLIENT: Yes.

COACH: Yes. What else would you notice, besides the feeling or the certainty that everything is now working as you had hoped?

CLIENT: Yes, that I also have the (...) that I have a balance between the things that I like to do and between the things, let's say, that have to be done.

COACH: Okay. The mandatory, the must-do program ...

CLIENT: Exactly, the must-do program. That I simply have a good way of dealing with the must-do category as well.

COACH: What else is different?
CLIENT: (…) After a relaxed breakfast, I drive to the office or to the appointment or do my job in a relaxed way.
COACH: Good. Then you're in the office. What happens there?
CLIENT: There are the things to do that I like to do and like to do a lot. Then there are also the things to do that are in the must-do category, that I don't like doing so much, but that have to be done. And in my, what did you call it, wildest hopes, I then have a good distribution on such a day. And when I go out in the evening, I have also completed my mandatory program.
COACH: And when a day runs just like that, how exactly do you behave in the office?
CLIENT: I think there will have been a change in my attitude. That I don't put off the annoying mandatory program until the next day, but that I simply give it a place and don't feel that it's something annoying that has to be done now. But, yes, my attitude to this topic would be different.
COACH: And if your attitude is different, how will other people see that your attitude has changed?
CLIENT: (…) Yeah, they will just notice that I was …, I don't know, writing minutes or sorting folders or filing things for 2 hours.
COACH: So they will already see the difference?
CLIENT: Absolutely. They'd see that I'm working constantly—without lots of getting up and down and making coffee or going to the bakery quickly or stuff like that … just doing it now. That's how they would see it.
COACH: Okay. Cool. What else are they going to notice?
CLIENT: They might see that relaxed smile afterwards when it's done. I just know that feeling when you've worked through something like that, that you just say, wow, I've done it! I've done that thing I've been putting off for 3 weeks, now it's done.
COACH: Does that show on your face?
CLIENT: Exactly. You can see that in my face.
COACH: Okay. Let's go through the day a little bit like this. What else happens in the office during the day?
CLIENT: (…) Yes. I think that I also, when I … when I get stuff done, I'm just in a better mood. And unforeseen, unpleasant things that suddenly come from the outside—I can deal with more easily. (…) I am friendlier. I am probably nicer. I get much less upset.

COACH: What are you doing instead?
CLIENT: (…) Maybe I'm just very relaxed about dealing with unpleasant situations or any confrontations or any unpleasant conversations. Like with product suppliers or actually, yes, probably with everyone I communicate with. So my brother, who is in the office with me, who's sitting right across from me, would hear it directly. As would the other colleague who is also in the office. So the three of us in the office would definitely notice. And then ultimately the people I communicate with. Which is 99% by phone.
COACH: Okay. What's next?
CLIENT: Yes. I'd have a good lunch break, a good meal, without any stress. And then a coffee after that. Back again. (…) Things would feel well done, well processed. I'd have a good feeling, I'd earned my money! Then I'd shut down the computer without any stress, go home. Let's assume it's one of those days where there's still commitments in the evening. No matter whether the highway is full or not or whether the train is coming on time or not. I'd just put in a CD and drive home. I'd still have time to maybe eat a sandwich, pack my bag and, in good time, without stress, I don't know, go to training or whatever in the evening.
… to be continued!

Fifty Questions Around Goals and the Preferred Future

The questions listed here are intended as a suggestion and to show the many possibilities of solution-focused questions. The collection does not follow a fixed structure but revolves around the preferred future that the clients would like to achieve.

1. What is the goal of our work?
2. What do you expect from the coaching?
3. What would it take today for you to be able to say at the end of our meeting that it was worth it?
4. What is the one thing that you want to change as a result of our coaching?
5. Imagine we work together successful and then you say goodbye and you go home. What do you tell your partner at home? What was particularly helpful for you?

6. Imagine we are 5 years into the future. How did you manage to deal better with today's situation? What was helpful for you back then?
7. What dream would you like to fulfill with the coaching?
8. What is the maximum target achievement for our collaboration?
9. How will you know that the coaching was successful for you?
10. What will be a change you would be happy with?
11. What will be a good outcome for our coaching?
12. What will be different if the coaching was successful?
13. What benefits can be expected if the desired future is achieved?
14. From today's discussion, what would you like to take with you into your hoped-for future?
15. How will you know we can finish the coaching?
16. How will I know we can finish the coaching?
17. Who else could tell me that the coaching can be finished?
18. What will this person use to determine that the coaching can end?
19. This is a difficult situation. What do you want instead?
20. What is most important to you about changing the situation?
21. How will a change affect your life?
22. What recent examples have gone somewhat in the desired direction?
23. What do you enjoy most about work (or any other relevant situation)?
24. What are you particularly good at?
25. What do you want instead?
26. What is the future you envision?
27. Please paint me a picture of your preferred future.
28. What does your ideal day look like?
29. How do you behave on an ideal day compared to today?
30. Imagine that a miracle happens overnight, and the problem disappears. How will you know the next morning that the miracle has happened?
31. How do you notice in your behavior that the miracle has happened?
32. Imagine that I watch a movie about the day after the miracle. What exactly will I see?
33. How will your perception change once the miracle happened?
34. How will your relationships change if the miracle happened?
35. Who else notices that the miracle has happened?
36. How will your view of yourself change?
37. How will your best friend/your partner/your boss/your colleague/your baker/ … notice that the miracle has happened?

38. How will you react differently to your best friend …?
39. How will your best friend … react differently?
40. What will your best friend (and others) tell me if they were to describe what the situation would look like without the problem?
41. What will be the impact of its disappearance?
42. What will be the best thing about the problem being gone?
43. What will have changed in your behavior?
44. What other changes would your changed behavior cause?
45. How will your perception of the environment change?
46. What difference will this make?
47. Who else would notice the difference?
48. What are your best hopes from our work together? (BRIEF London).
49. Assuming your best hope has been met or exceeded, what is different and how is it different? (Solution Surfers, CH).
50. What is your best hope for the impact of our conversation for your everyday life? (Solution Surfers, CH).

3.3 Recognize and Develop Resources

The following describes the second phase of SCF, the identification and development of a client's resources. The goal is to increase the client's awareness that they have all the resources they need to achieve their goals. The following methods are used for this purpose:

- Resource questions
- Positive exceptions and signs of progress
- Scale questions
- As-if frame
- Compliments

From the talk about the preferred future, there is a seamless transition to identifying the client's existing resources. The easiest way to learn about these resources is to ask about them:

> - "What signs have you already seen in the last few weeks that point in the desired direction (preferred future)?"
> - "At what point have you been able to experience a little bit of the miracle?"
> - "What other progress has there been?"
> - "What has already worked?"
> - "When has it been a little better than usual?"
> - "What else?"

Together with the clients, we explore the first signs of the preferred future and thereby jointly gain insights into resources (behaviors, thoughts, emotions, social support) that already bring clients a little closer towards their preferred future. Of course, it does not stop at describing these initial signs, but rather exploring HOW they got there. How did the clients manage to create these positive signs? Through the dialogue about the first signs and movements in the desired direction, the awareness is strengthened in clients that they have already done something that leads them in the right direction, that they are competent and can do something on their own to further approach their goals. This enforces the client's self-efficacy beliefs, which are strengthened through dialogue about their own share in the progress they have already made. The self-efficacy beliefs, according to Bandura, are a central prerequisite for clients to consistently pursue further steps towards the goal. Supporting the process is to visualize the mentioned resources and behaviors that are perceived as helpful. This keeps them constantly present and makes it easy to work with them as the conversation progresses. By describing the positive signs of the preferred future and the client's associated behaviors, the relevant skills that the clients must have to exhibit the behaviors automatically become visible. For the coach, the described behaviors thus provide further indications of resources that can be useful in achieving the goal. At the same time, they are the basis for compliments that the coach makes to clients about their activities, abilities, efforts, etc.

Compliments aim at the same effect as discussing the positive signs: Raising awareness and strengthening the client's self-efficacy belief. Therefore, compliments are not polite niceties, but always refer to very concrete and comprehensible efforts and behaviors of clients, which are important for achieving the goal. Only then can these compliments have the desired effect.

Once the behaviors are conscious and comprehensible, the question of what is necessary to repeat or expand these behaviors arises almost automatically. The goal is to use the positive approaches in the client's own behavior and thinking to get closer to the preferred future. Here SFC becomes resource talk, which strengthens the client's self-efficacy beliefs more and more. In SFC, both the self-confidence and the view of the client's own competencies grow. Eventually—and probably sooner rather than later—clients no longer need the coach as a counterpart but can then continue the process towards the goal on their own. However, we are not yet there. Before that, we use scale questions, which have become popular through the solution-focused approach, to focus on what has been achieved by the clients so far.

Scale Questions

By describing the preferred future, we have already defined 10 on a scale from 0–10. When working with scales in SFC (see Sect. 4.2 for a detailed description), 0 usually stands for the situation in which the clients decided to go to coaching or just as the opposite of 10. The 10 stands for the fact that the preferred future has been fully achieved.

> "On a scale of 0–10, where 0 represents the situation in which you decided to go into coaching, and 10 represents that you have fully achieved your preferred future, where are you today?"

In other words, the 10 is the answer to the miracle question or the description of the preferred future. The 0 does not need to be described further intensively, since that would only lead to the problem talk. Often it is enough to define the 0 as "the opposite" of 10. The fact that this definition is vague is not a problem for the further process. The important thing is to concentrate on the 10! For the recognition of existing resources, the coach now asks where on the scale clients see themself today. In my coaching practice, it has never happened to me that the clients gave 10, 0, or even minus 1 as an answer. So usually, a number between 0 and 10 is given. And with that step alone, clients have done something that has brought them from 0 towards 10. It is irrelevant whether clients mention 0, 5, 3, 4, or X as status. Since we as coaches as well cannot know exactly what a 3 or X means in the client's world, the number mentioned is not that important. What is important is to know how the clients have managed to reach this status. In this way, together with the clients, we get to the resources that have been used so far. Any distance from 0, no matter how small, is equivalent to resources that clients have used.

Even if clients would call the 0 or even talk about a minus 2, the question is how they managed not to slip even further down the scale or to keep the 0. This also requires resources, of which clients should be aware. By describing the difference from 0 to 2, 3, or X, we get information about the positive signs for progress and can work with these resources accordingly. Very often, it is enough for clients to become aware of their own resources, which they have been using rather unconsciously. Through the awareness of having these resources at their disposal and being able to use them in a targeted manner, many clients already find their way back into their own ability to act. To support clients even further on the path to 10, however, the as-if framework already mentioned can also be used.

Use As-is Framework for Resource Development

Like using the as-if framework to describe the goal ("How in your behavior will you know the miracle has happened?"), you can also use this approach to describe the next step on the scale. Since we don't usually jump from level X on the scale to 10, the point is to use the scale to break down the big goal into smaller, more manageable goals that are more likely to be achieved. So the question now is:

> *"If you have moved one step further on the scale, how can you say that you are now at the X + 1 level of the scale?" ... What else?"*
> *"What difference does it make? ... What else?"*
> *"Who else will know the difference? ... Who else?"*

The description of signs for changes is at the same time a description of the next small step towards 10, i.e., towards the preferred future. Again, we never ask "What will be the next step?" because this is the question most clients have difficulties to answer. We ask, "How can you say that you are at the x+1 level on the scale?" or "What are the signs that tell you that you've moved up the scale on to the next level?" This way clients describe to themselves what the possible next steps could be.

Thus, an essential intermediate goal in coaching has been achieved. Clients have an idea about the situation without the problem, they can describe their preferred future, have explored positive signs of progress, have reported how they made it to the scale value X and can even describe how they will notice that they have reached the scale value X + 1 (or just 0.5). With this, we are approaching the end of the first and maybe even final coaching session. Therefore, at this point, it is usually useful to mirror back to clients all the constructive things they have done so far.

Transcript of Real-Life Example: Continuation

COACH: Okay. Get to your training in the gym stress-free, arriving with time to spare, that would be a successful day. So, if you take that as a reference and now think back a bit over the last few days and weeks, was there a moment were you first felt that that things were starting to move in this direction?

CLIENT: Yes, there was. That was where I actually got up earlier in the morning!

COACH: Okay.

CLIENT: Yes. And before that, whilst I don't want to claim I was playing high-level sport, I was starting to do more regular exercise.

COACH: So that was already going in that direction?

CLIENT: Yes, exactly.

COACH: What else?

CLIENT: What also happened is that I started making more customer appointments, so the first live customer appointments, a little later. That immediately made me feel more relaxed.

COACH: (…) What else?

CLIENT: What else? Yes, that I actually (laughs) update my calendar for the month or for the week …. That I name the, let's say, the annoying things, that I really name them and block time in the week and say, so, that's when I'm going to do the painful stuff.

COACH: And that has already happened?

CLIENT: Yes. That's already happened, sometimes it worked on that day. But (laughs) sometimes you end up moving it over from Tuesday to Wednesday. Then you just don't do it on that day. But that's O.K. … .

COACH: As an approach in the right direction. So there were blocked times for the annoying things, even if they were not always worked on every day.

CLIENT: Yes.

COACH: Okay. Good. So, let's keep these things in mind. You know, there are these wonderful scales. Like this one. From zero to ten. Ten would be your best hope. At ten you have implemented everything as you have described today and zero would simply be the complete opposite.

CLIENT: Okay. Yes.

COACH: Where are you today on this scale of one to ten?

CLIENT: Today? Three or so.

COACH: How did you do that? How did you manage to get on a three?

CLIENT: (…) Self-discipline. (laughs)—How did I manage that? (…) I just did it. I just did it.

COACH: Okay.

CLIENT: Yes. So, initially out of sheer necessity, but I think it was also out of the desire to do something differently. That I don't take on so many things for 1 day anymore, but that I limit it a little bit. Yes, I think I'm more conscientious with it, because I set the priorities.

COACH: Okay. How do you do that? How are you more conscientious about it?

CLIENT: In that I sort out, for example, mentally or perhaps also with a sheet of paper, what are really the to-dos for this day that have to be done. And that I, yes, deal with it more conscientiously, with more discipline. And that I don't let myself be distracted so often by "Come on, let's postpone that until tomorrow."

COACH: Yeah, OK. What else are you currently doing to get to the three on the scale?

CLIENT: I talk about it, for example. The fact that I'm sitting here now contributes to the fact that I'm on three, that I also talk about it with my partner. That I'm discussing it with my office colleagues. And, yes, just the fact of looking at what possibilities or what solutions there can be simply makes things more pleasant.

COACH: Okay. So, you're talking to the people around you who are also affected by it all. Okay. So just doing less, sorting things, talking to others about it. It's quite a lot. What else?

CLIENT: Is there anything else on the three? I can't think of anything now …

COACH: Okay. Good. Anyway, that's quite a bit. The goal is, after all, the ten. Usually, we don't jump right from the three to the ten. Ten is where we want to go or where you want to go. And so the safe way is in a series of smaller steps, I would say. If we take, let's say, one scale step, from three to four. How will you know that you've reached a four?

CLIENT: (…) How would I notice that? I think I would notice that when I can regularly get up earlier in the morning. Without thinking that I haven't slept enough or that I would like to do something different now. I get up and am happy that the day is starting.

COACH: Beyond that?

CLIENT: (…) Yes. I think, on days like that, I might just go outside for half an hour for a break. Yes. In between times. Just to get a little fresh air or something.

COACH: Okay. So, if you just think through what you've said up to this point. Your best hope, the ideal day, the signs that you're on a four, that something has changed towards a ten. What goes through your mind when you review this?

CLIENT: Well, what's been going around in me all the time, I'll say, is that I've often thought that in the evening, late at night, I just go to bed too late and then usually watch something totally stupid, which doesn't give me any energy at all. And that I just eliminate that and just get going a little bit earlier in the morning and rather do some sports in the morning and start the day more relaxed …

That I change how I deal with unloved issues and consider what I can delegate if necessary. (laughs) And yes, how I can reward myself when I do that. So that would be worthwhile to look into more.

Fifty Questions to Recognize and Develop Resources

1. What signs in the last week were there that went in the desired direction (preferred future)?
2. At what point could you already experience a little bit of the miracle?
3. What other progress has there been?
4. When has it been a little better than usual?

5. What has already worked?
6. How did you deal with similar situations in the past?
7. What were your recipes for success from the past?
8. What positive changes have been noticed by friends (partner, boss, etc.)?
9. What have you been happy about in the last few weeks?
10. What else has this progress changed?
11. What other changes have supported this progress?
12. What does it say about you that you have made this progress?
13. What skills did you use to make this progress?
14. Where were there exceptions to the current problem?
15. When was it less bad than usual?
16. When did the problem take a break?
17. What have you done to pause the problem?
18. How did you manage to give the problem a rest?
19. If the last few weeks were a movie, what would I see in that movie that led to this change?
20. What role would you have in this film?
21. What are your character's strengths (in the film) that led to the progress being made?
22. What other characters in the film would I see as being supportive?
23. What happens next in this movie as it moves towards a happy ending?
24. Let us assume that you make further progress. What does that progress look like then?
25. Which of your skills can you use in addition to maintain progress?
26. What behaviors have you seen that have had a positive impact?
27. What gave you hope/confidence?
28. What change have given you hope/confidence?
29. What makes you think progress is feasible?
30. What is the best thing about the successes so far?
31. On a scale of 0–10, where 0 represents the situation in which you decided to go into coaching and 10 represents achieving your preferred future. Where are you today?
32. What does this number X mean?
33. What are you most excited about now that you are at X?
34. How do you behave at X?
35. What goes through your mind when you think about the fact that you are now already at X?

36. How do you feel about X?
37. What is better with X compared to X-1?
38. How did you manage to get from X-1 to X?
39. What changes have you made?
40. When you are one step further on the scale, how can you say that you are now at the X + 1 level of the scale? ... What else?
41. What sign will tell you that you have reached X + 1?
42. How do you know that you have taken this step?
43. How confident are you that you can/will take that smallest next step?
44. What difference will that make? ... What else?
45. How will this difference spur further change?
46. Who else will notice the difference? ... Who else?
47. Who will support you in taking the next small step? ... Who else?
48. How will these people support you in taking the next step?
49. What do you do to get those people to support you in taking the next step?
50. What other changes will be triggered by this move?

3.4 Recognize and Reinforce Progress

> This part of SFC describes the follow-up session. It is about making the changes since the last meeting visible and usable to strengthen clients on their way to their preferred future. It is possible that this second session never takes place, as the coaching may well be completed with the previous session. If it does take place, these are the steps of the follow-up session, in overview:
>
> - Creating a positive past
> - Making differences visible
> - Taking responsibility for success
> - Using scale questions and as-if frames
> - Ensuring implementation in everyday life
> - Giving compliments

Create a Positive Past

If clients have decided to come to another session, the session continues with the identification and development of resources. The pre-assumption that change will happen in any case is expanded in a solution-focused way to the pre-assumption that change has occurred in a desired direction. Accordingly, the first question in the follow-up session is:

> "What has changed for the better since we last met?"

This question helps clients to create and talk about a positive past. We direct the focus to the positive changes and thus to the client's resources that were necessary for the changes. So we are back to the joint search and awareness of the resources that have ensured that the clients have come a little closer to 10. The question about the change that happened is somehow the "little brother" to the question about the positive signs of the desired future. By focusing on a positive past, we highlight the aspects of the past that worked and can, therefore, serve as a pattern for further progress towards 10.

Positive Differences Are Made Visible

To further explore progress and its consequences, we then ask about the differences that brought about the changes:

> "What impact have these improvements had?"
> "What difference did those impacts make?"
> "Who noticed the difference?"
> "What other changes have occurred as a result of these differences/improvements?"

The more detailed description supports the awareness of the client's own resources, sharpens the view for the positive changes and strengthens the motivation for the further path towards to 10.

Take Responsibility for the Successes

Describing the positive past and the differences or successes created does not automatically result in clients perceiving themselves as the source of change. Therefore, the solution-focused coach supports this process with the following questions:

> "How did you behave differently so that these improvements occurred?"
> What else joker
> "How did you do that?"
> "What skills/strengths/behaviors did you use to bring about this change/improvement?"
> What else joker

Scale Question and as-if Framework

Analogous to the first session, one can continue to evoke differences and changes with the scale question.

> "Where on the scale are you now in relation to your goal?"
> "How do you behave differently? How else?"
> "What difference does it make? What else?"
> "Who notices the difference? Who else?"

With each answer in the direction of X + 1, clients describe aspects that are now working better. Both the question about the improvements and the scale question are asked to understand how clients have managed the changes. The coach always targets the behavioral level to get a concrete description of what resources the clients have available to get closer to 10.

In the further course of the follow-up session, the procedure of the first session already described above is practically repeated by asking in the as-if frame for the description of the next step on the scale:

> "If you are one step ahead on the scale, how can you say that you are now at the X+1 level of the scale?" ... What else?"
> "What are the first signs of such a change? ... What else?"
> "Who else will know the difference? ... Who else?"

With the description of the next scale level, the clarification of the next step, this session would also end. But before ending the session, and ideally after the clients have described the resources that have enabled them to go to the next scale level, the coach should express appreciation for what the clients have accomplished. In other words, compliments are given here as well, as described earlier under the heading "Recognizing and Developing Resources."

Summary of the Follow-Up Session
To describe the basic procedure of the follow-up session, it can also be summarized in six steps:

> 1. On a scale of 0–10 and with a view to your desired change: Where do you already stand today?
> 2. How did you manage to get there? What-else joker
> 3. What is different when you are one step ahead? What-else joker
> 4. What do you do differently when you are one step ahead? What-else joker
> 5. What do you do next? What-else joker (question 5 is optional)
> 6. Compliments

Almost 50 Questions Around Progress

Most of the questions on the creating a positive past section are identical to the questions on the positive signs of a preferred future and therefore will not be repeated. In the following, only the questions that are explicitly mentioned in the section as examples and questions that result from working with the scale are listed. Thus, what follows here are not 50 new questions, but 30 questions plus the questions from the section recognizing and developing resources.

1. What has changed for the better since we last met?
2. What impact have these improvements had?
3. What difference did these impacts make?
4. Who noticed the difference?
5. What other changes have resulted from these differences/improvements?
6. How did you behave differently so that these improvements occurred?

7. How did you manage that?
8. What skills/strengths/behaviors did you use to bring about this change/improvement?
9. How do you behave differently? How else?
10. What difference does it make? What else?
11. Who notices the difference? Who else?
12. Where on the scale are you now in relation to your goal?
13. How have you managed to stay at X consistently?
14. How did you manage to stay at X and not slip back again?
15. How did you manage to stay at X-1 instead of sliding to X-2? (X-3, X-4, … -1X, -2X, …)
16. What helped you stay at X (-1)?
17. Who helped you stay at X (-1)?
18. What skills do you use to keep from sliding back down?
19. How do you use these skills?
20. What else can using your skills kick-off?
21. If I were to talk to your best friend (partner, boss, etc.) about the time since we last met, what skills/strengths could they tell me about that you have used?
22. If I were to talk to your best friend (partner, spouse, boss, etc.) about the time since we last met, what would they tell me about how you have been able to maintain a constant X?
23. If I were to talk to your best friend (partner, boss, etc.) about the time since we last met, what would they tell me about how you were able to avoid slipping further than X-1 on the scale?
24. How do you manage to stay on the ball even though X has not changed?
25. How do you manage to stay motivated even though X has dropped to X-1?
26. What does it say about you that you stay motivated/on the ball even though successes have not come as quickly as you had hoped?
27. How did you manage to get here today?
28. Since you have already been to X, you also know how you behave on X. What exactly do you do differently than compared to today?

29. Since you have already been to X, you also know how you perceive things differently at X. How do you perceive things differently at X compared to today?
30. *See "Recognizing and developing resources" above:* If you are one step ahead on the scale, how do you know you are now at the X + 1 level of the scale? Etc.

3.5 Adjourning

> This last phase of SFC ends the collaboration for the moment. This phase may already take place at the end of the first session. There are different opinions about the concrete procedure, even among solution-focused coaches. What most solution-focused coaches agree on is that compliments are given to the clients at the end. In addition, one could...
>
> (a) ... try to secure the next steps by an action plan.
> (b) ... make suggestions for behavioral experiments to support further goal achievement.
> (c) ... ask clients to define their next steps to strengthen their clarity and commitment to proceed.
> (d) ... mention the trust you have that clients know best what to do next and that they will do what is best for them in the current situation.
>
> It may well be that one solution-focused coach pursues one or the other of these approaches and another solution-oriented coach pursues different approaches. Of course, all these approaches have their justification. Practitioners should find out for themselves which approach is the most helpful for their clients.

Approach A (action plan) will certainly suit many people from the business context, as it is familiar to them from countless meetings and workshops. Approach A provides coaches and clients with a description of who does what with whom and by when. If this is the expectation of clients, then this approach can certainly have a motivating effect on them.

At the same time, it may well be that there are circumstances that stand in the way of implementing such a concrete plan, as has been experienced hundreds of times after team workshops from business, which can quickly lead to frustration over the failed plan. On the other hand, it meets the expectations of many clients, as this is how they envision a well-rounded conclusion: A concrete action plan that can best be synchronized with their outlook calendar or activity list in their smartphone.

Approach B (behavioral experiment) was classically used in SFBT to help clients have new experiences. Towards the end of a therapy session, there was often a pause, the therapist would withdraw and think about appropriate compliments and "homework" for the time until the next session. Then the therapy session continued, the compliments were shared, and the task was presented as a suggestion. In a therapy or even coaching session, however, suggestions from the consultant are rarely rejected, as this would be almost close to breaking the rapport, which clients are very reluctant to risk doing. Therefore, such suggestions are usually accepted by clients. In coaching today, one speaks less of homework and more of behavioral experiments. As useful as these may be, they direct the focus to the behavioral ideas of the coach for the clients. Therefore, the question arises as to what the additional benefit is for clients if they have already described in the previous step what the next meaningful steps are. Moreover, we assume that the coach is not in the position to know better what is useful for clients than themselves. Therefore, if a behavioral experiment is suggested by the coach at the end of a session, it should not in any way compete with clients' ideas about their next steps. Almost always suitable is the Formula First Session Task, an observation task for clients, presented in Sect. 4.3, that directs the focus of perception to positive aspects in the client's life.

Approach C (self-commitment) is a kind of explicit commitment and implementation review of the next steps with clients. This can be done by asking clients to summarize what they take away from the coaching session and what the next steps are. This summary can be backed up by scales for the probability of implementing the next steps and the clarity of the next concrete actions. Both the probability and the clarity about the next concrete steps should be as high as possible. If this is not the case, clients are obviously still missing something to take the next step towards the preferred future.

> 1. *"Once again, please imagine a scale of 0–10 that you can use to assess the likelihood that you will actually make these next steps a reality. 10 is very likely and 0 stands for very unlikely. What do you think the probability is?"*
> 2. *"Once again, please imagine a scale from 0–10 that you can use to assess clarity about next steps. 10 represents very clear and unambiguous and 1 represents completely unclear steps. How high do you rate the clarity about the next steps?"*

Approach C would conclude by asking if there is anything else the clients need to be able to tackle the next step. If this last question is answered in the negative by the clients, the session ends with compliments to the clients.

This leaves approach D (trust). This approach assumes that the question of the next steps and whether the clients need anything else to address them is unnecessary. What clients also do not need is a behavioral experiment suggested by the coach. Our clients have described what will be different on the next scale level and hence know themselves what the next step can be. Whether the next step is then implemented in this or another form depends on many factors, but certainly not on a task given at the end of the coaching. After all, the change has already begun with the clarity about the preferred future, the recognition of the positive signs and the awareness of self-efficacy. Now clients are trusted to use their existing skills and resources to do what is useful for them in the given situation. So at this juncture, all that remains for the coach to do is to repeat the compliments once again, to thank our clients for the cooperation and trust placed in the coach, and to wish them all the best. This procedure is certainly the most consistent way to end a solution-focused coaching.

> *"I am impressed by the clarity with which you have described signs for progress. To me, both your assessment of your progress to date and of the possible next steps sound very realistic. I would like to take this opportunity to thank you very much for the cooperation so far and wish you every success for the further steps towards your goal! Thank you!"*

Whether another session should take place after this conversation is decided only by the clients. Often the procedure described above is sufficient to provoke a small change in behavior or even experience, which in turn brings about further changes. As already described in the basic assumptions, the solution-focused work assumes that small changes can be sufficient to get sufficiently strong momentum towards the target state. That a change happens cannot be prevented anyway. It also becomes clear here why solution-focused coaching can be ended after just 1 hour.

3.6 Mastering Challenging Situations

> This section addresses situations in which the offer of solution focusing cannot yet be accepted by the clients. That is, when questions about positive exceptions, improvements, resources, and goals are all answered negatively. For this purpose, we distinguish three relationship dynamics in SFC:
>
> - Customer relationship
> - Complainant relationship
> - Visitor relationship
>
> Depending on the relationship dynamics, coach and client have different ways of working together. In addition, linguistic possibilities are shown to address specific difficult situations.

Relationship between Coaching Client and Coach
Whether a client can engage in solution-focused coaching depends largely on the relationship between client and coach. In SFC, there are three types of relationships or patterns we can distinguish. It is important here to emphasize the relationship type and not the client type. Relationship describes the dynamic between coach and client that builds up over a period. This says nothing about the personality of the client or the coach. This also says nothing about a possible change in the relationship dynamic between the two people, which of course can change at any time. It is simply a description of a current dynamic that has implications for what the coach is offering the client at the present time. Many SF coaches reject even this classification by relationship type, which is quite understandable. However, here we fall back on this concept to describe

situations in which the process of SFC does not work as smoothly as we would like. It also helps us to be better prepared for such situations.

1. *Customer relationship*: Clients have a clear desire for change and a willingness to work actively on finding a solution. At the same time, clients are open to looking for their own share in finding and implementing a solution and to contributing accordingly. The approach of coach and clients is the joint work around the clients' goal and changes that will bring them closer to their preferred future. Thus, ideally, coach and client work together in the manner described throughout this chapter without any problems around the process of the SFC.
2. *Complainant relationship*: Clients in this relationship dynamic emphasize the problem and usually see the solution in others. Clients usually do not see themselves as part of the solution, but rather as a victim of external circumstances or third-party behaviors. The solution is for others to change. Consequently, the desire is for the coach to provide expert advice on how to get other people to change.

During a coaching session, which is characterized by a complaining relationship dynamic, the coach repeatedly invites clients to switch from describing the problem to describing the preferred future. It is of course a prerequisite that clients are taken seriously, and clients are given the necessary appreciation:

Appreciation and Invitation to the Solution Talk

> Coach: "You gave me a truly clear and detailed description of the situation and the people involved. Thank you for that! I can see that the situation must be incredibly stressful for you and I understand why you are here. My question now is what do you want instead?"
> Client: "XY simply has to behave more fairly. He needs to understand and respond to me. Also, he needs to treat me with more respect."
> Coach: "Suppose by some miracle XY behaves fairly and respectfully toward you, how would you respond?"
> Client: "Well, that would have to be a big miracle ... But if he really behaved decently, then of course I would be able to behave differently!"
> Coach: "How exactly might you behave then, if you behaved differently?" ... .

Of course, with this little sequence, the problem talk would not completely disappear. It will probably take several attempts by the coach to get from problem talk to solution talk. And since problem and goal are independent of each other, the central question that can be asked repeatedly is:

> "What do you want instead?"

Positive Intent and Other Conversation Starters
It is thus the core of the miracle question that reappears in the most varied form in the questions about the preferred future. For this invitation to be accepted, the ground must be prepared with appreciation. To do this, it is important for the coach to hear the positive intention behind the complaints. After all, a basic systemic assumption is that all human behavior has a positive intention, and that each person behaves in a way that seems reasonable to them. So, when clients complain in the first place, they want to achieve something positive. What is this positive? To be heard? Expression of a particular value? A desire for change? Whatever it is, it is worth mirroring to the clients, demonstrating that their positive intention is valued. Thus, the client's intention is not questioned, only an alternative way to fulfill the positive intention is sought together.

Additional conversation starters for this kind of dynamic are based on the basic assumptions in Chap. 2:

1. You do not have to fix what isn't broken.

    (a) "What's working today, despite all the problems you've described?"

2. Doing what works should be done more often.

    (a) "When did it work out a little better than you just described?"

3. If something does not work, you should try something else.

    (a) "I think I understood what didn't work out. So we don't need to repeat that. Maybe we can consider what has not been tried yet. "

4. Small steps can lead to big changes.
   (a) "This sounds like a big job. Perhaps the task is a bit too large and confusing now. What might we think of instead as the first small step toward change?"
5. The preferred future is not related to the problem.
   (a) "Let us leave Mr. XY out of this for the moment. How do you generally imagine a good working day?"
6. The language of solution development is different from that required for problem description.
   (a) "Thank you for the detailed description of the problem. It became clear to me that you have developed great competence in dealing with the situation. Can you please explain to me in more detail how you manage to deal with the situation?"
7. There are always signs of the preferred future.
   (a) "I understood that the situation is unbearable. It must be incredibly stressful. In what few moments might it be a little less stressful than usual?"
8. The future is both something created and something negotiable.
   (a) "Going back to why you came here, what exactly do you want to accomplish by working together?"

The pattern of these approaches to conversation should now have become clear: Take complaints seriously—appreciate the positive intention—use the positive intention. The heritage of Erickson's hypnotherapeutic approach can be clearly seen here. Everything our clients offer us in coaching can also be used to support them in achieving their goals. And since clients have a lot to report in this special client-coach relationship, we as coaches also have many starting points to do just that.

3. *Visitor relationship*: Sometimes clients are also sent to coaching because, for example, their supervisor thinks they should change. The superior is thus the complainer in the relationship dynamic. But since

we have no mandate to work with the superior, we are now sitting across from a client who has no problem, no goal, and no expectation of change—at least not at the beginning of the coaching. The goal is to reach a common understanding of the situation and an attractive goal to work on. In coaching, it is often possible to begin with an initial three-way conversation when the client and contract partner (e.g., supervisor, HR representative) are not identical. The goal of the conversation is then to establish the general goals of the coaching. Regardless of whether the client shares the supervisor's goals or not, this initial discussion can be taken as a starting point for further work.

> *"If I have understood you correctly, you cannot understand your boss's point of view. You see no need to work even better with your colleagues. What do you think would be worth discussing in our coaching instead?"*

Here, too, we apply a similar approach to coaching with the complainant relationship pattern: appreciation and invitations to solution talk. Very often the relationship dynamic changes from visitor to complainant. This is because clients have been sent by someone who perceives them as "deficient," which is usually rejected as an evaluation. We therefore do not work on the supervisor's attribution of the problem to the client, but rather pick up the client's perception of the situation. This enables the necessary relationship building, which helps initiate and make possible a change from the complainant relationship pattern to, eventually, a customer relationship pattern.

Challenging Answers and Questions from Clients

Of course, challenging situations in SFC always include verbal reactions from the clients that were not expected in this way. Below are some typical answers/questions from clients, with possible reactions from the coach. Whether the respective answer of the coach makes sense depends of course mainly on the relationship to the client and the concrete situation. The answers here are therefore intended to stimulate one's own imagination rather than to be understood as a set of ready-made recipes.

Client: I don't know how I would know that a miracle has happened! How would I notice that?
Coach: What would be there instead of the problem?/How would an ideal day look for you?
Client: I don't know!
Coach: It is a difficult question, I know. In which direction would your answer go if you knew?
Client: I don't know what I want, that's why I'm here!
Coach: The answer to the question is also a significant one, of course, which requires a little more time. What is, so far, already a little clearer?
Client: What would you do if you were me?
Coach: I would be happy to give you my personal assessment of the situation later. Before that, however, I would be interested in your -perspective.
Client: I have no idea. Surely you know similar situations. What can you think of?
Coach: I would be happy to share my experience with you. But to avoid me making suggestions that you have already tried and discarded, I would first be interested to know what you have already tried …. Which of these approaches has worked best?
Client: There were no improvements. On the contrary! Everything has become worse.
Coach: Where exactly on the scale of 0–10 do you stand today? … How have you managed not to slide down even further? (see Sect. 3.3 Recognizing and reinforcing progress)

Most responses result from the application of the basic assumptions and an unconditional appreciation of the clients. Clients always have a good reason to react the way they do. Therefore, the client's questions are not a form of "resistance" to the coaching, the questions or even the coach. Rather, they indicate to us the need for a different approach or also for more appreciation.

4

It Is More than a Miracle

4.1 The Miracle Question and Its Children

Steve de Shazer has often pointed out that the miracle question was given a small blemish at birth when it was called the Miracle *Question,* since it is not really a question in the true sense of the word. It is actually more of a dialogue between client and counselor that follows the problem talk and moves the focus to the solution. The client should be supported in designing a future without reference to the problem. However, as a goal, the simple absence of the problem is not enough on its own. More importantly, a concrete picture of what the client wants instead for the future should emerge. After the development of the miracle question, this intervention quickly became an integral part of every SF conversation. The goal is to let clients develop a picture of what their world will look like when they have reached their preferred future. The clearer the picture, the clearer the steps are that they must take to achieve that future. The following are typical steps in this dialogue as used by Steve de Shazer and Insoo Kim Berg.

Invitation to an Experiment

I would like to ask you a somewhat strange question. A question that may require some imagination to answer.

Pause to build tension and wait for the client's reaction.

Introduction of the Question

Imagine that after we finish our session today, you go home, do the things you usually do, have dinner, maybe watch a little TV, and so on. At some point you go to bed.

Pause so that the client can imagine the situation.

The Miracle and the Question

While you are asleep, a miracle happens ... The miracle is that the problem you are here for today is solved. Just like that ...

Pause for effect

However, you do not yet know that the problem is solved, since you were asleep.

Pause for effect

Now, when you wake up in the morning, how will you first realize that the miracle has happened?

Pause, pause, pause—The client needs time to think, which should not be interrupted by further questions. Even if clients put a little bit too much imagination into their answer ("It's raining roses from the sky ... ") the coach should not say anything yet but wait until the client describes the change a bit more realistically.

Exploration of the Miracle

- *How else would you know?*
- *How will your best friend know that the miracle has happened to you?*
- *How in your behavior will your friend (partner, colleague, boss ...) notice that something is different?*
- *Who else will notice? By what?*
- *That is a very big miracle! What might be the first little thing that will make you realize that the problem is gone?*
- *When xy is gone, what do you do instead?*

Of course, these questions are not simply asked one after the other. As I said, this is about a dialogue and the answers need time. Allow your clients time to imagine the situation concretely and then answer. If there is no answer, keep silent (6 second rule) instead of asking the next question right away.

Working with the Miracle

Once the miracle has been described in detail and concretely, further work on the preferred future follows, as described in the previous chapters.

Over time, another question has developed in the field of SF work that has a similar goal as the miracle question. As mentioned briefly in Sect. 3.2, Chris Iveson and colleagues from BRIEF, London, ask their clients right at the beginning of the session, "What are your best hopes from our work together?" From the start, this question prevents clients from engaging in problem talk and getting caught up in their usual loop of presenting problems. By answering the question, the client automatically provides a description of their preferred future and thus moves straight to the solution talk phase. Building on the answer, Peter Szabó and Daniel

Maier (Solution Surfer, CH) take the client's response to the best-hope question further, "Assuming your best hope has been fulfilled or exceeded, in what way are things different?"

The question is designed to highlight the concrete differences between today and the preferred future in our daily life. These differences are explored in more depth, so that we attain an even more detailed description of the preferred future and a clearer idea about the consequences this would have on daily life.

4.2 Scale Questions

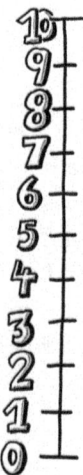

According to de Shazer, the scale question was not invented by him or any of the other therapists at the BFTC at all, but simply taken from work with clients. One or the other client began to rate their assessment of the situation or their state of mind on a scale from 0–10. Since this way of describing things turned out to be extremely helpful, this question was adopted and further developed—true to the motto: If something works, do more of it!

The scale questions can be best used after clients have described their preferred future, be it through the miracle question or the best hope question. If the exchange about the miracle or best hope is so clear and vivid that the coaching client and the coach have a good idea of the situation, then it is time for the scale question. The description of the preferred future then represents the top of the scale, the 10. The 0, on the other hand, is usually defined as the time when the client decided to go into coaching or just the opposite of 10. It is not necessary to ask for the worst possible situation. It is sufficient to choose a point in time when the issue was still predominantly defined as a problem and not too long ago. The numbers themselves don't say much anyway. What does it mean if clients say that they are at a 6 regarding the goal? Is that good or bad? Are they happy with it or depressed about it? What does the 6 tell us? What resources are linked to it? What path does the client still see ahead? The scale is just a vehicle in the communication and makes it easier to talk about the preferred future, sub-goals, differences, resources, and signs of next levels, meaning progress, on the scale. Here is an example:

> On a scale of 0–10, where 0 represents the situation in which you decided to go into coaching, and 10 represents that the miracle we talked about has occurred. Where are you today?

Now the client usually names a number that is above the lowest scale point. It doesn't matter whether the client is talking about a 1.5 or a 5 or any other number. What is important is to ask specifically what this number represents and what resources are associated with reaching this number.

> O.k. So you are at a 3 today. How do you determine that you are at a 3? How did you manage to get to a 3? What else did you do? What else? What else? ...

The point here is to create awareness that clients have used resources that have taken them from 0 to X number. On the one hand, this emphasizes clients' powers of self-efficacy, which are important for motivating them to continue pursuing their plans for the future. On the other hand, opportunities are already hidden here to do even more of what is good for the client. The description given by the client reveals resources that can be used for further work. But this is not the end of the scale question, because it now goes on to break down the goal and turn it into smaller, easier to achieve goals.

> Now, if you go up a little bit on the scale, say from the 4 to the 5–o.k.? How can you say that you are on the 5? What are signs of improvement? What will be different then?

In answering the question, clients automatically describe a sub-goal that brings them closer to their preferred future. At the same time, clients also anticipate signs of progress, ensuring that they won't miss them when they actually happen. The important thing here is not to ask in the subjunctive, meaning using "What *will* you do differently if you were at 5?" and not "What *would* you do differently of you were at a 5?" Because, after all, this is exactly the question that the client has often asked themself and can't answer. *"If I knew what I could do differently, I wouldn't be here ..."* Therefore, you let clients describe how they realize that they are one step further and then work with this description of the near future/ the next step.

Just as with the miracle question, you can also ask the scale question more precisely about reaching the next level by introducing a third-party:

> How will your best friend know you have taken a step forward? How will your boss notice ... etc.

In summary, scales serve ...

1. ... the clarification and/or the visualization of an assessment (means of communication)
2. ... the differentiation of a point of view (good—bad vs. from 1–10 or even 100)
3. ... the development of sub-goals
4. ... the discovery (by description) of the next steps
5. ... the description of progress

The last point "description of progress" should be explicitly discussed again here, since this is practically the introduction to the following session. Scales are also an excellent way to follow up on the last session.

> *Looking at your preferred future, which is 10 on our scale, where do you stand today?*

This way you are back to talking about changes, behaviors, successes, etc. Even if the number on the scale is lower than it was at the end of the last session, you can ask, "How did you manage to move down only one level in this situation instead of going down two or even three levels?" Incidentally, this would also be the question the coach can ask if a zero is given as an answer in the first scale question. Again, one can ask how the client managed not to slide down even further. Or how the client mustered the strength to show up for the coaching appointment even though they are at the 0 today. Resources are always there; you just have to see them—and scales help!

The effects of scales on clients can be many and varied. As a rule, working with scales supports clients' solution focus, promotes their motivation and confidence, and prepares them for the next steps. In addition, scales can be used to ask about the …

- … proximity to the preferred future
- … quality of the relationship with the coach
- … quality of the relationship between people in general
- … satisfaction with the process (or a situation, development, etc.)
- … confidence about the success
- … extent of hope about something changing for the better
- … willingness to act
- … clarity about the next steps
- … progress since a point X in the past (e.g., last meeting)
- … all forms of change (development in a relationship, closeness to the goal, etc.)
- … assessment of own creativity (strength, patience, will …)

- ... extent of certain moods and emotions (dejection, optimism, relaxation, aggression, etc.)

As you can see, there are no limits to your imagination here. Develop your own way of dealing with scales. I would like to give you one more idea, which I got from Peter Szabó and Daniel Meier: On a scale, not only individual points can be marked, but also areas. Clients often find it difficult to commit to a single level. Sometimes it is like this and other times like that. Then, of course, you can take a perceived average value. However, you can also offer clients to define a range, in which, for example, their confidence about the possibilities for change is currently located. In this way, you build a bridge for clients to use the scale without reluctantly having to commit to a single level.

At the same time, I can again ask about the difference it makes when the client is at the upper end of such a scale range. Analogously, I can also use ranges on the scale in the follow-up sessions, making it easier for the client to describe their progress:

> *Since our last meeting, there have certainly been changes that have sometimes gone in the desired direction, but perhaps also sometimes in an undesired direction. Now, if you take our scale of 1–10, which value marks a situation that was furthest away from your goal? And which value marks a situation that was closest to your goal?*

You allow the clients to talk about the highs and lows of the recent past, but then proceed with the attention focused, as usual, on the positive side and explore what was different at the highest point on the scale. How have they managed to get there, And what else? What else? What else?

4.3 Formula First Session Task and Compliments

At the beginning of the book, an anecdote described one of the founding moments of the solution-focused approach, when a family was advised to pay attention to what should not change in their lives over the next 2 weeks. This is exactly what the Formula First Session Task (FFST) is! The FFST is a task for clients that for a while was given as a standard task at the end of the first session. The goal of the task is to shift the client's focus away from the problem and towards available resources. Steve de Shazer phrased the question as follows:

> Between now and next time we meet, we [I] want you to observe, so that you can tell us (me) next time, what happens in your [pick one: family, life, marriage, relationship] that you want to continue to have happen.

In addition to greater clarity about their personal goals and resources, the task is also intended to increase optimism about the client's own abilities to achieve goals. The certainty of being able to influence things positively (self-efficacy) is a central point in the motivation of change processes. As a rule, the task has the effect of turning an originally rather negative view of the situation into a more differentiated view. This alone generates strength for dealing with the situation or the intended change. At the same time, the reported positive aspects of the current life situation are resources that can be used for further change. Be it because clients themselves notice more starting points for change, because the broadening of perspective has made new possibilities visible, or simply because clients can approach the next steps with more confidence.

Compliments

This confidence and the increase of the self-efficacy perception is promoted by another aspect, which is used at the end of the session: compliments! Clients are usually too busy with their problems to see what they have already achieved and how well they have dealt with certain issues. However, the coach in SFC has a central focus on exactly these things and listens carefully. Therefore, at the end of a session, it is quite easy to highlight aspects that clients perceive as compliments. It is important that compliments always refer to specific observations of the clients' strengths and resources. A simple "you're doing great" usually does not convince clients and may even be understood as a devaluation. Compliments should be based on observations made by the coach that clients can also relate to.

> *"I am impressed by the creativity with which you are looking for a solution. You have produced a lot of ideas today on how to make your working environment more satisfying and have also already described which of your strengths you will specifically use to achieve this. I am equally impressed by the determination with which you want to try new things. You have set yourself three specific measures that you will implement within the next 2 weeks. In my view, that's a very promising start!"*

Right now, after the compliments, the FFST described above comes into play:

> *"In addition to all the planned changes, until our next meeting, I would like to ask you to observe what there is in your work, life and your social environment that you would like to keep the same. What do you want to keep the way it is, because it's good for you?"*

Finally, we will briefly discuss why this step is called Formula First Session Task. To do this, it is helpful to understand that in the tradition of the original brief family therapy, a very precisely planned intervention (often in the form of a task to the family) was placed at the end of each session. An entire team of therapists thought about this. The goal was to design an intervention that was just as unique and to the point as the family's unique problem itself. So here, for the complicated lock, the key that fits exactly should be found. Later, the Milan School of family therapy sought more standardized forms of intervention. This was taken up by de Shazer and his colleagues and they developed an intervention that was the same for all clients and was independent of the problem—just a lock pick called FFST.

Today, the FFST is not only asked at the end of the first session, but sometimes even before the first session. Since the initial contact often takes place on the phone, clients can already be encouraged at this point to pay attention to everything that is already going in the right direction, is helpful or has perhaps already improved, until the first meeting. This considers the observation that many changes in the direction of the goal already begin when the decision for a coaching has been made. In the first session, you can then use these positive impulses and the resources for the coaching. Since changes always happen (in life nothing stays the same), a natural process is used, and the focus for observation is moved to the positive aspects of the general changes in life.

4.4 Attentional Focus

SF works strongly with conscious attention directing. In SFC, through our questions, we repeatedly focus the client's attention to their preferred future, past successes, their own resources, and the resources in their social environment. The FFST is a good example of this. We ask clients to consciously pay attention to the aspects in their lives that are going well and are working. The compliments we give as coaches are another good example of how we also consciously direct our attention to positive aspects of the client's behavior. So we can distinguish attention directing in the client and also in the coach:

The Client
We can draw a client's attention to positive aspects of their life with the following questions, amongst others:

- Questions about the preferred future.
- Questions about the first signs of the preferred future in the present.
- Differences, which are expected by the occurrence of the preferred future.
- Question about the current progress towards the preferred future on a scale.
- Questions about the resources that have made this progress possible.
- Questions about successes or progress in the past.
- Asking for signs of further progress.
- Questions about possible changes after the coaching session.
- Questions about the likelihood of certain changes taking place.
- Questions about positive changes since a certain point in time (e.g., the first coaching session).

To be able to ask these and other questions, however, the coach's focus must of course already be on resources.

The Coach
Of course, the coach also focuses their attention on positive aspects of the client's behavior. To do this, the coach must first and foremost listen well. However, the SF coach does not listen in the sense of Active Listening, as defined, for example, by the International Coaching Federation: "The ability to focus completely on what the client is saying and is not saying, to understand the meaning of what is said in the context of the client's desires, and to support client self-expression." The SF Coach also focuses completely on what the client is saying, of course. However, the coach does not try to understand the meaning behind what the client is saying and is not saying. The SF coach, therefore, doesn't summarize everything that the client has said or might have meant, but consciously listens selectively for clues to the client's resources. So the SF coach listens specifically for strengths, skills, abilities, past successes, wishes for the future, social

resources, etc. We call this type of listening Constructive Listening (BRIEF London). We never assume that we can fully understand our clients, but we use aspects of what is said as an offer for clients to use these elements for their own goal achievement. That is, by directing the coach's attention to resources and sharing our observations, we in turn focus our client's attention on their own resources, which can be used as building blocks for their desired future.

For the coach, Constructive Listening also helps to hear resources behind a client's persistent complaining. For example, behind every complaint about a situation is a desire for change, a commitment to a cause or value, or even concern for a person. If clients did not care about a situation at all, they wouldn't complain about it, so complaining actually says something about a client's values and desires, which can be important in shaping their preferred future. This means, therefore, that coaches must focus their attention fully on their clients and their resources in everything they say.

Part II

Team Coaching: Reteaming®

5

It Is All About Motivation: Reteaming®

5.1 The Idea of Reteaming®

In the 1990s, Ben Furman, a Finnish psychiatrist, and his partner Tapani Ahola, a Finnish social psychologist, were increasingly asked by companies and organizations to advise them and provide them with consulting support. Both were already known and recognized as trainers for Solution-Focused Brief Therapy. In their work with organizations and teams, they then used the same principles and strategies they had followed in their work with individual clients and families: describing a preferred future, being aware of progress already made, setting achievable goals, looking at existing resources, and more. Furman and Ahola realized that the principles and strategies of SFBT, with only minor modifications, could serve them as a guide in working with teams and even organizations.

Furthermore, in the 1990s, working with the healthcare division of Finland's national oil company (Neste), they developed a step-by-step approach to coaching teams to optimize their collaboration and effectiveness. The goal of this project was to write an easy-to-use manual for coaching teams. The result was a process model with 12 clearly defined steps, which they called Reteaming. Reteaming has subsequently proven to be an extremely useful tool in working with teams in a wide variety of contexts, such as companies, public administrations, and non-governmental organizations.

Ben Furman and Tapani Ahola presented the 12-step process to colleagues in Finland as well as in other countries. It quickly became apparent that the path taken with Reteaming had a stronger appeal than the founders of the approach had initially suspected. In just a few years, Reteaming had spread not only to other Scandinavian countries, but also to other parts of Europe. Today, there are certified Reteaming coaches in many countries around the world, including Germany, Japan, China, and Indonesia. Reteaming coaches use the method in a wide variety of areas. The approach has proven to be a highly effective and at the same time, pragmatic guide for working with teams and organizations, but also with individuals, when it comes to transforming problems into goals and building the necessary motivation to achieve these goals.

What Is Special About Reteaming®?
In many organizations, people have a lot of experience with problem-oriented conversations and meetings. These conversations are typically led by the responsible manager or by an external facilitator. The goal is to get the problems on the table and discuss them in the group. The issue is that such discussions run a high risk of revolving around blame. The reason for this is that many people assume that the best way to solve problems is to analyze the problem and to identify what caused it. The search for the cause of the problem then leads to what are often understood as accusations, since every explanation for the causes of problems in the team is always associated with a potentially responsible person or group of people. This leads not only to quite natural defensive behavior, but very often to counter-explanations (counterattacks) and escalation. After all, no one wants to be held responsible as the cause of the team's problems.

The solution-focused approach avoids this unfortunate constellation of accusation, defense, and counteraccusation. If the focus is no longer on the problems and the attempt to find the cause of the problem, the atmosphere of the conversation changes significantly. "What do we want our future to look like as a team?" is a very different question than "What's not working and why isn't it working?" People prefer to talk about the desired future because it inspires hope in those involved. They listen to each other better when it is about the other person's dreams rather than their problems. Once team members listen to each other, they also become more open to seeing resources in each other and show more interest in each other's ideas and suggestions. Therefore, the main guiding idea for Reteaming workshops is:

> No one (solely) is responsible for the problem, but everyone is responsible for the solution!

The solution-focused approach generates positive energy in the system that leads to new creative ideas and ways of working together. It does this through its focus on hope for a better future, progress already made, resources within and outside the team, small steps towards change, promises to contribute to positive change, and a follow-up on progress. Reteaming can be viewed as a coaching method that is particularly suited to collaborative problem solving. It is a pragmatic tool for teams and groups that are working together in search of constructive problem solving and/or ways to improve collaboration.

5.2 The Five Factors of Motivation

Motivation is a complex concept and fills entire volumes of psychological literature. With the aim of conveying central aspects of motivational psychology, the founders of Reteaming have taken the liberty of translating some core elements of various motivational theories into five central factors of motivation. These factors are, of course, a strong simplification of the psychological concept of motivation, yet they are not far from what recognized scientists tell us about this topic.

First, we assume that it is difficult to be motivated if there is no clear and desirable goal. Once such a goal is in place, we can think about what people need to generate the necessary energy, interest, will, persistence, and perseverance to do what is necessary to achieve the goal. For this purpose, Reteaming proposes the following factors that are necessary to build motivation.

1. Ownership: It is your goal!
2. Desirability: The target is attractive to you.
3. Confidence: You have confidence in your ability to achieve the goal.
4. Success: You experience progress towards the goal.
5. Perseverance: You do not give up in the face of setbacks.

If you put the five factors into a metaphorical formula, it looks like this:

$$M = O \times D \times C \times Pm \times Ssb$$

The Reteaming formula thus states that the motivation to change (M) arises from an own, attractive goal (*Ownership* × *Desirability*) times confidence in success (*Confidence*) times progress monitoring (Pm), which makes the successes visible, times strategies against setbacks (Ssb). Of course, this is not a mathematical formula, but rather a metaphor, which we use in team workshops to make the elements for successful change visible. However, what does correspond to a mathematical formula is that all variables must be greater than zero so that the result (motivation for change) is also bigger than zero. Let us now take a closer look at the five factors.

Ownership
People are more motivated when it comes to achieving their own goals! This means goals they have set for themselves, rather than goals set for them by others. Reteaming takes exactly this into account. In the Reteaming process, goals are not predetermined. Instead, participants in a Reteaming workshop are invited to think about their own desired future or an attractive team vision.

Another way to develop your own goals is to ask participants to make a list of current problems and then help them transform them—problem by problem—into goals. This is another way people arrive at their own goals instead of having to work on someone else's. After all *a problem is only the flip side of a goal*. However, in Reteaming we prefer to work with goals, so we transform every problem into a goal.

At the same time, individuals and teams in organizations are not always in a position to set their own goals completely freely, as organizational goals have to be taken into account. This means that there must be an overarching framework for goal setting in organizations, even if it would be ideal from a motivational point of view to be able to determine one's own goals completely independently. This circumstance must also be considered in team coaching à la Reteaming.

Desirability

In Reteaming, we pay close attention to the attractiveness of the goal: "Is the goal significant? Is it important? What will be the positive effects of achieving the goal? What positive consequences will the goal have for oneself and others?" The reason for focusing on attractiveness is simple: the greater the perceived benefits, and therefore the attractiveness, of the goal, the more desirable and interesting it becomes to participants. Once a goal is defined, it is worth spending some time identifying the various positive effects that achieving the goal will have on the individual, the team, and the organization. Team discussion on the benefits is important, as some team members may already be convinced of the goal and its benefits, while other team members may not yet be able to see what achieving the goal will bring them. Collectively gathering benefits of goal achievement helps ensure that all participants in the group see the advantages of pursuing the goal together.

Confidence

You have determined the goal yourself or together in the team. You are convinced that achieving the goal will bring many benefits and will pay off. Nevertheless, this is often not enough to activate your motivation. You usually also need to believe that achieving the goal is possible and that it is also possible for you as an individual. Therefore, in Reteaming we take care to build confidence and actively look for evidence that the goal is not only attractive, but also achievable. The following factors give us confidence in our success:

1. You are aware of your own resources.
2. You have supporters in your team, and outside your team.

3. You can see the progress you have already made now, so you are not starting from scratch.
4. You can visualize your further progress in small steps that build on each other.

These four elements of confidence are integral parts of the Reteaming process. We ask people to reflect on what progress they have already made towards their goal and what helpful skills, competencies, or resources they can identify on the team. We ask them to imagine the small steps they will take and the people they can ask for support in achieving their goal. This also makes it obvious that confidence in success, along with the attractiveness of the goal, are the foundations of Reteaming.

Success

Motivation can be generated by one's own goal and its attractiveness as well as confidence in success. At the same time, this motivation will be short-lived if it is not reinforced by the experience of success and progress. If this component of the motivation equation is eliminated, all other components lose their power. It is important to make sure that people get the feeling of making progress and achieving success. If this feeling is missing, it can quickly cause their initial motivation to diminish or even die out during the process. For this reason, in the Reteaming process, we consciously pay attention to both large and small signs of progress towards the goal. We highlight these signs, analyze them, give credit to the team for making progress, and thank everyone involved for their contributions. Acknowledging past successes, progress, and contributions to goal achievement is a key element in team coaching in the spirit of Reteaming.

However, people tend to overlook their past successes. This is where the coach plays an important role. By asking questions like, "What progress have you made so far? What else has happened that you are happy with? What else? How do you explain the positive change? How did you do it? How have your colleagues supported you in this? How does it feel to you?" the coach supports the recognition of past successes. These and similar questions are the coach's tools of the trade. With them, light is shed on what is important for maintaining motivation.

Perseverance

In an ideal world, progress would be a linear process in which things would simply get better and better. In reality, however, progress is rarely that linear; it tends to follow the rule "two steps forward and one step back."

In other words, possible setbacks in the process are foreseeable. They are even unavoidable and are part of the overall process. Therefore, they should be expected instead of trying to avoid them altogether. It is good to be optimistic and believe in progress, but at the same time, it is important to remain realistic. Successful change is the result of a combination of optimism and realism. Optimism, without the willingness to deal with setbacks, is even risky. It can lead to loss of motivation as soon as setbacks happen. For this reason, the Reteaming process explicitly addresses dealing with setbacks. The goal of this step is not to fear the worst and think about all the conceivable obstacles that could occur on the way to the goal. Rather, it is a matter of realizing that unexpected setbacks may occur and mentally preparing for them. In this way, one achieves a kind of protective vaccination against the demoralizing effect of possible setbacks.

In summary, we can say that Reteaming is based on a simplified theory of motivation. According to this, motivation is not just either there or absent. It is a dynamic driving force that depends on certain factors that can be influenced through coaching and conversations. The stronger people feel that the goal is also their goal, the greater the benefits promised by achieving the goal, the greater the confidence in success, the more clearly progress is perceived, and the better prepared people are to deal with possible setbacks, the more likely it is that the team has already done and, in the future, will continue to do everything it can to embrace change and achieve its goal.

6

It Starts with a Motto: The Assignment

6.1 The First Contact

Before any team coaching, there is the first contact between the team lead and the coach. This usually takes place by telephone or by e-mail. If the contact is made by e-mail, this probably only serves to organize an initial contact by telephone. An exchange about the matter and the general conditions via e-mail is rather difficult and would raise more questions than it could provide answers. Therefore, we concentrate here on the initial contact by telephone. The goal of the initial contact for the potential client is usually to find out whether you are a suitable coach and what the team coaching process might look like. The first question won't be adequately answered over the phone; this usually requires personal contact in person or video call. You should be able to answer the second question in simple and clear terms. After all, you are the expert on the process and since the question doesn't come as a surprise, you can be prepared accordingly. A possible answer to the question can be found below. First, let us look at the goals for the initial phone contact from our perspective, from the coach's perspective. At the end of the conversation, the following goals should have been achieved:

1. To clarify for yourself whether you would like to accept the assignment or not.
2. To gain an impression of the organizational setup and the reason for the team coaching.
3. To agree on an appointment for a personal get together.

To do this, you can clarify the following questions during the phone call:

- Who is the caller? So that you know in which role the caller is contacting you.
- What is the reason for the call? So that you get an initial orientation in terms of content.
- Who knows about this call? So that you can assess what the information status of the parties involved is.
- How many people and organizational units are involved? So that you can get an idea of the scope of the team coaching.
- What has been done so far on the issue at hand? To give you an initial assessment of the history of possible previous solution attempts.

This information should be sufficient to be able to assess on the phone whether this is an inquiry that you would like to work on. Above all, the information serves for a first impression whether it is a request for team coaching or, e.g., mediation. Potential clients ask for team coaching or team development and mean a wide variety of things: growing together as a team, dissolving tensions, dealing with change, reorganization after an organizational change, accompanying the team through a special phase in the organization or team development, conflict mediation within the team or conflict mediation between the team and team lead. Team coaching in the sense of Reteaming is suitable without further ado for all of these situations, apart from mediation. Of course, there are also solution-focused mediations, and Reteaming can also serve well in these cases. At the same time, however, additional skills are needed to conduct team mediations, which are not covered in this book. So we remain here in the broad field of collaborative processing of team issues and the further development of the team itself.

If you have gained the impression during the telephone call that the topic, the industry, the company, or the number of people involved is not what you would like to do, then give the caller advice on where they could find someone suitable. This can be from your own network or perhaps a reference to a coaching association that you are close to.

But we assume here that the inquiry sounds like it is exactly what you like doing. Then it is time to describe your general way of working to the caller, i.e., to answer the question about the process. Of course, you do not yet have enough information to go into detail about everything that is important to the inquirer, but you are able to describe how "usually" the process might be.

> **Example**
>
> Thank you for this first impression on Team XY. You had asked how I would approach the topic, and I would like to briefly address that. As a rule, the next step is a personal meeting between us, where we can discuss the further procedure in detail and you can get an impression whether you want to work with me as a person. I will be able to learn more about the team and the people involved during the conversation. If we conclude that we want to work together, we will then try to establish a joint approach to the team coaching/team development/ …?
>
> The most important thing for me is to understand the exact goal and orientation of the workshop. We will transform the general goal of the workshop into a kind of motto under which the workshop should take place.
>
> The workshop as a central part of the team coaching will last between one and a half and 2 days. It is important that the workshop can take place in a quiet, undisturbed atmosphere outside the organization. The overnight stay plays an essential role. For one thing, individuals or groups often come up with things overnight that can be worked on during the second day. If we conclude such a workshop within 1 day, we run the risk that the necessary need for discussion cannot be adequately addressed the next day. In addition, an evening together in a pleasant atmosphere is often an important positive group experience that supports the team process. How we will continue to work after the workshop, for example, and when a review should take place, is something we will discuss together in the workshop.
>
> The entire workshop will focus on creating constructive ways and approaches for the future. We will certainly also briefly look into the past, but we won't spend a lot of time discussing team history. This is often time and energy consuming and doesn't bring us much closer to the desired future. It will be much more important to get an agreement on what we want to achieve in the future. At the end of the workshop, there will be concrete agreements on how the team wants to proceed. The focus is on small steps that can definitely be implemented successfully, rather than big changes and upheavals that could quickly overwhelm the team.
>
> Finally, I will document the workshop using a photo log and debrief with you. That is the general procedure for such a workshop.

If the inquirer (client) has further questions, these will of course be answered. It is now important to decide whether to arrange a first personal meeting or not.

What if it Is Not the Team Lead Calling?

Let us now turn to the second case, which often takes place during the first contact: You get a call from the HR department of the organization concerned. This can be the HR management, an HR business partner, or an HR development specialist from the organization. This depends on the size and structure of the organization. Depending on which type of HR person calls, you can expect to have different levels of prior knowledge regarding team coaching or team development. Whereas more prior knowledge doesn't always have to be advantageous, the more knowledge the HR professional has, the clearer their picture will be of what team coaching should look like. Should that match your understanding, there is no problem. However, if the understanding is different, you will first have to convince them that you really know what you are talking about and of the benefits of the Reteaming approach.

In any case, it is important to clarify in which role the HR person is calling. To find a suitable coach or facilitator and then withdraw from the process? As a contractual partner? Does the HR person want to be involved in the entire process? When an HR person calls, it is often the case that they want to be involved in at least the initial meeting with the team lead. At this point, at the latest, it is important to clarify what role the HR person will play. As a rule, representatives of the HR department should not take part in the workshop because they are not part of the team, represent the employer's perspective due to their role, and are associated with disciplinary measures in the eyes of many employees (warnings, entries in the personnel record, etc.), which usually does not promote openness in discussions.

However, what is just as important for the caller from the HR department as it is for the team lead is the description of your general approach in team coaching. The goal of the conversation should also be a personal meeting with the team lead and, if requested by the client, the HR person.

6.2 The Personal First Contact

An initial personal meeting has been arranged and you will meet the team lead. As a rule, the meeting begins with another personal introduction. You can introduce yourself and your experience, and the team lead will answer with a personal introduction. It can be quite helpful for you to learn how experienced your counterpart is, how long the manager has been leading the team and whether there are any special team constellations that have a part to play in the current situation.

The introduction of the team lead often transitions quite seamlessly into the description of the situation and the team. It is helpful here if you have an organizational chart with the names of all team members. If this is not quick to print out, the manager can usually draw this quickly on a piece of paper. The point is not so much to describe individuals in detail, but to understand the nature of the collaboration and mutual dependencies. Here, one can focus on the competencies and resources of the team. This gives the team lead an immediate impression of what is important to you and how you work.

The goal is not to do an initial team diagnosis or to figure out the team's problems. It is about getting a first picture of who you will meet in the workshop. This can be important in terms of room design, planning group work with appropriate material (number of flip charts …) as well as the possibilities to form sub-teams if there are many different topics that are only of interest to parts of the group. So it is more about the data for the design of the framework and less about content information for an analysis of the team situation.

After you have understood the basic team constellation, the next step is to clarify what exactly the goal of the team coaching should be. This can vary depending on the initial trigger for the workshop. Here are some typical examples:

- Clarification and elimination of tensions among team members
- Concrete agreement on improved cooperation
- Visible support of all team members for the new beginning

In addition to the goals for the workshop, it is equally important that the team's lead understands that the workshop itself will only initiate a process that will then continue into the day-to-day work of the team.

> **Example**
>
> "If we assume that the workshop was successful and concrete agreements were reached, it is important that this positive momentum is then maintained. This task remains with the team, but above all, with you as team lead. I can gladly support you and the team in a review if that is desired. However, the actual change should take place in daily life and this is promoted by focusing attention on the positive changes after the workshop. This corresponds to our basic orientation for such workshops, that we rather look forward and focus on the positive approaches in the team. If we try to clarify the causes of current problems in the workshop, it usually results in individual team members feeling attacked, defending themselves and thus dropping out of the joint search for solutions. They can only really get back on board when the accusation of guilt—no matter how it is disguised—no longer exists. If the question of guilt remains in the room, the blame game starts all over again, which is a vicious circle that doesn't help the team move forward. We will therefore focus early on in the workshop on the desired future of the team, quickly translating existing problems into goals and finding out which common goals seem worthwhile for the team. When we focus on a goal, there are no more culprits, no more blaming. There are only team members contributing positively towards achieving the goal."

Here, the team lead will certainly have one or two more questions. Ultimately, the team lead wants to feel that they are in good hands and that you are up to the task. Therefore, it is important that you can speak authentically about your experiences, but also about the possibilities and limitations of such a workshop. Furthermore, a simplified visualization can also make clear the advantages of a solution-focused over a problem-focused approach, which can be used to explain the basic philosophy of the workshop.

6 It Starts with a Motto: The Assignment

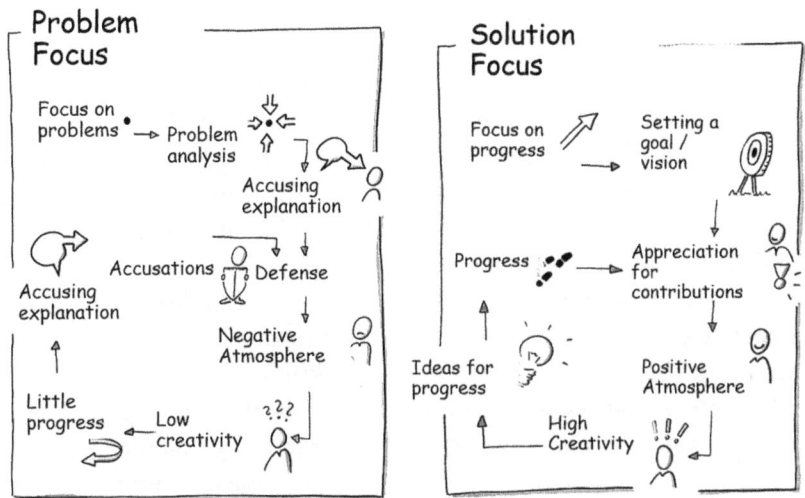

Flip charts: Problem focus, Solution focus

If the team lead agrees in principle to the proposed path, you then need to talk about the motto of the team workshop. The motto provides the content framework for the event. It therefore defines the general topic without restricting the participants in their goal setting during the workshop. Therefore, the motto should

- Be generic
- Have the future in mind and
- Be formulated positively

A good example of a motto is: "Together for better teamwork!" or "Together to the top!" "From good to great!"

It is also important that the motto specifies a topic that can also be worked on and directly influenced by the team. For example, you can certainly discuss whether you should change the company's strategy or whether it would be good to hire 100 more people, but both topics are probably outside the team's sphere of influence—unless you are talking about the company's board of directors as a team. We need a motto that provides a positive frame for the workshop and describes a preferred future for the team. The motto is created by the team lead and should be approved by the team before the workshop or at the beginning of the workshop. However, it is not necessary to discuss it in detail with the entire team before the workshop begins. Of course, it is okay if you do not come to a finished version of the motto during the initial contact, this can also happen following the meeting. The important thing is that the motto is ready in time to be included in the invitation to the team members, because it is a key part of the invitation.

Once you have agreed on a motto, you and the team lead can organize the next steps. The team lead's task is to inform the workshop participants about the date and motto of the workshop. Send the team lead a short profile of yourself and your web address so that the team members can find out more about you without having to use a search engine.

Your task as a facilitator is to send a final proposal, including a generic agenda for the workshop, to the team lead.

Agenda
- *Welcome*
- *Introductions with a Difference*
- *Review of The Workshop Motto*
- *Our Vision*
- *Target Focus*
- *Benefit Check*
- *Resource Collection*
- *Next Steps*
- *Strategies against Setbacks*

Such an agenda always depends a little on the specific objective and the starting position of the team and can therefore vary. However, it shouldn't be too detailed and, above all, should not include precise times. Both would restrict you too much as a coach. Also, not all 12 steps of reteaming are listed, so that you can flexibly respond to the team process in the sequence and the design.

7

It Is About the Team's Future: The Team Coaching Workshop

7.1 Joining

The beginning of the workshop focuses on the joining phase, similar to an individual coaching, and the orientation of the team members. Joining means that a positive initial relationship is established between the coach and the team members to ensure a constructive working environment right from the start. In this context, the basic atmosphere in the Reteaming workshop is of particular importance. For the solution-focused approach to be experienced right away, we begin with a special kind of personal introduction after the coach's own brief introduction. This often takes place before the agenda is presented and before possible "rules of the game" for the workshop are laid down.

> **Example**
> "My name is Joerg Middendorf. I am a psychologist specialized in organizational psychology and live with my family in Cologne. I originally worked as an HR specialist in industry, where I worked in HR development. Subsequently, I worked as an internal coach for an international management consultancy. So working with people and especially with teams on a variety of occasions has accompanied me all my professional life.
> Before I say something about the workshop in general, the agenda and the organization of the workshop, I would like to know something about you."

This already creates the transition to the team members. The aim of this short self-introduction is that within the first few minutes of the workshop, each team member should have spoken aloud to the group, giving them the chance to relax and be noticed by the others. It therefore makes sense that you, as the facilitator, do not speak for too long yourself in order to let the team members have their say at this point. It is usually not advisable to use the classic expectations question, since too little has been said so far about the framework and the prepared agenda. Instead, the importance of a solution focus should already be made tangible at this point:

> **Example**
> "I would now like to ask you to introduce yourself. But don't worry, you don't have to say very much at this stage, please just tell me your name and your function. Everything else will be told to me by your colleagues here in the room. We will start with you right here at the front. After you have told me your name and your function in the team, I'd like to ask the others to tell me two or three of your strengths that we might use during the rest of the workshop. It doesn't have to be all your strengths—that would probably take too long. Two or three strengths per person are enough for a first impression. Good, then we'll start with you. O.K.? Your name is?"

The first person in the circle of chairs begins and states his or her name and function. Then as coach, look slowly at everyone the circle and wait until the first strengths are mentioned. Often there are three, four or more strengths that are raised. Do not let the list of strengths get too long (no more than five), as this can increase the pressure unnecessarily for the others in the group. During this round of introductions, it is often the first time ever that team members hear publicly, from their teammates, what they are valued for. This introductory exercise alone is a special experience for most team members and makes them realize that this workshop might be a little different than the team's previous workshops. Curiosity and openness are encouraged and prepare the ground for further action. As a coach, you can just listen to the introduction and the various strengths of the team members or you can collect all the strengths that are mentioned on a flip chart. This way you have already a nice collection of team strengths that you can use later.

After briefly thanking the group for engaging in this first exercise, you will now introduce the philosophy of the workshop:

Example

"As you have noticed from this round of introductions, this workshop puts a special focus on the things that everyone can contribute positively to the overall success of the event. In addition, the title [= the motto] of the workshop also points towards the future "Working even better together". Throughout the workshop, we will not look back and see what hasn't worked until now, but we will look forward and discuss how we want to work together and what everyone can contribute to the future.

I'd like to explain this approach right away with the help of two flip charts [see above figures Problem Focus and Solution Focus]. But first, imagine that your car has broken down. Hot, white steam is hissing out of the engine, which is clearly not running properly. A mechanic takes a closer look at the problem and concludes that the cylinder head gasket is broken. She replaces the gasket, and the engine starts ticking over smoothly again. Problem solved! This approach is familiar to most of us: We have a problem, we look for the cause, and having found it we then solve the problem. This often works very well—but typically only with machines. With people, it tends to work less well.

Please look at this flip chart [see figure Problem focus]. We are trained to spot errors and see problems. Once we have discovered a problem, we analyze it to find the root cause. Like in our example with the engine. But in teams, this leads us to finding an explanation for the problem, which automatically implies an accusation. "Sales didn't implement the specifications, the back office service didn't prepare the material correctly, IT doesn't understand the business, the Marketing Department doesn't understand IT, top management lives in an ivory tower, middle management blocks everything, employees are resistant to change, etc."I assume that you are familiar with similar stories. Those addressed in this way naturally reject some or all of the accusation or explanation for the problem and start defending themselves, typically with a counter-explanation or with a counter-accusation. This leads to a negative mood, less creativity and thus little progress. After a short time, the search for the reasons for the lack of progress continues. Once the reasons have been found, the vicious circle of problem orientation begins again with another accusatory explanation …

We would like to dispense with the search for the guilty party today and therefore take a solution-focused approach [see figure Solution Focus]. Right from the start, we focus on progress and the development of a common team vision, a target picture of the desired future. Once we have agreed on this vision, we consider together who can contribute to it and where we have already made progress in heading in the direction of the desired future. This usually leads to a better atmosphere, higher creativity, sustainable approaches to solutions and the corresponding progress, as well as recognition for the contributions to this progress. We have arrived at solution focus! This is also a lot of work, but it's definitely more fun and sustainable than the problem-focused approach.

I would like to conclude the explanation of the workshop approach with a quote from Ben Furman and Tapani Ahola, who developed this approach: "No one is solely responsible for the problem, but everyone is responsible for the solution".

Flip chart: Everyone is responsible for the solution

This short presentation will help the participants to better understand all further activities during the workshop.

The goal of this phase is to get general agreement on the workshop philosophy, without a lengthy and detailed discussion of principles about the approach itself. Very often, the approach is quickly accepted. If there are more lasting doubts, you can also ask the group to view this an *experiment* and trust you as the facilitator and coach of the event regarding the method. During the workshop, most participants very quickly realize the benefits of this approach. At the same time, there will sometimes be individual participants who are reluctant to abandon their usual problem-focused approach. In that case, it usually helps to bring the concerns to the group and not to enter a dialogue with the skeptics. If one goes too quickly into dialogue with the people who are expressing sustained concerns, other participants may sit back and watch the spectacle. If, on the other hand, you take up the concerns and ask the group for their opinion, the group's desire for the solution-focused approach usually comes out clearly, making it easier for even the skeptics to engage in the experiment.

7 It Is About the Team's Future: The Team Coaching Workshop

This introduction of the workshop philosophy is followed by a brief and joint definition of the rules of the game for the workshop, so that all participants have what feels like a safe framework for the event. Typical rules of the game are:

- Confidentiality on all personal issues
- Respectful interaction with each other
- Cell phones are only used during breaks

In the sense of a common working basis, all rules are written down that are important to participants and for which there is no veto from other participants. Collecting the rules often takes only about 5 minutes. The agenda is then presented, and the workshop motto is approved.

Agenda and Motto

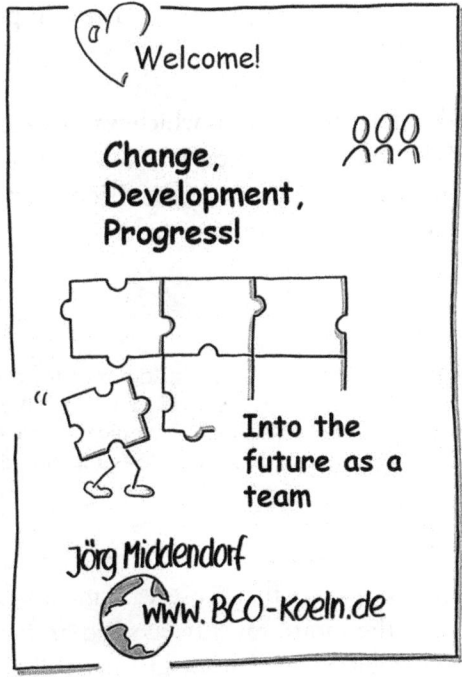

Flip chart: Welcome

The welcome poster is also part of the introduction, as it contains the title/the motto of the event. This title has been discussed in advance with the team lead. It is the motto already mentioned (in the invitation?), under which the entire workshop should stand. The motto should be positive, future-oriented, and generally applicable, so that all team members can identify with it. In nine out of ten cases, it is something like "Improve collaboration." There are several reasons for this:

- This title is open-ended enough to appeal to all team members and not explicitly exclude anyone.
- At the beginning, the team lead has little idea of what the workshop will be like and can therefore only choose a fairly broad title for the event.
- Although the trigger for doing the workshop was a somewhat negative one (We need to do better ...!), the welcome poster should reflect a positive orientation and it is usually about the team, its cooperation (coordination, communication, etc.) and an improvement of all these aspects.

This motto is a kind of pre-contract, which was only discussed between the team lead and the team coach. Now it is necessary to verify or change this pre-contract with the whole team. The vision of the team will then be developed based on the common motto.

> **Example**
> "The motto of your workshop is "Working together for a better future". What that means exactly and what it should look like will be clarified during our workshop. But before we start, I would like to hear from you whether the motto makes sense to you or whether it should be changed?"

Often enough, there is general agreement, because the motto is broad enough and sufficiently positive that most team members can relate to it. If this is not the case, the motto must be worked on further. Only then can the common team vision be developed (that will be the next step).

However, I have not yet encountered a request to change the motto. The title/motto probably doesn't have enough significance for it to be that controversial at the beginning of such a workshop. On the other hand, the desire for a concrete introduction to the workshop work is all the greater. So, we continue with the presentation of the agenda. As a rule, the agenda is so general that we have enough space to remain flexible about precise structure during the workshop.

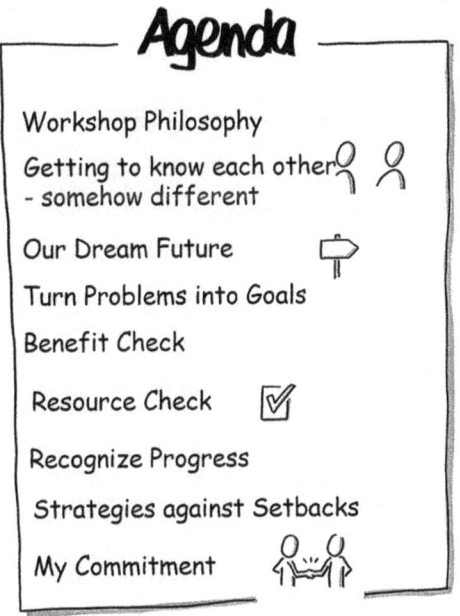

Flip chart: Agenda

Nevertheless, there should of course be room for questions and/or comments that you address. It is important in such a workshop that unnecessary speed or operational hectic is taken out at the beginning, making it easier for all participants to adjust to the special atmosphere of the workshop. On the other hand, this can also test the patience of team members who are particularly results oriented and want to move the process along quickly. The best way to keep these team members on board is by pointing out the clear structure of the workshop.

7.2 Start Checklist: Flip Charts and Material to Start With

- Two flip chart holders on which the following content is distributed:
- Flip chart: Welcome
- Flip chart: Problem and solution focus
- Flip chart: "No one is (solely) responsible for the problem, but everyone is responsible for the solution."
- Flip chart: Rules of the game
- Flip chart: Agenda
- Use tape to put flip charts that have been presented on the wall for documentation

8

It Is Only 12 Steps: The Team Coaching Workshop

8.1 Our Future Dream

Solution-Focused Coaching is always coaching towards the preferred future. Therefore, it is only consistent that we start exactly where we mean to go …. into the future! So it's no accident that this step in Reteaming is like the first step in SF individual coaching. There, we begin by asking, "What are your best hopes from our discussion today?"

In the dialog that follows, the client's preferred future is then worked out in detail, step by step. Of course, in team coaching, we must take group dynamic processes and group motivation into account. To do this, we first focus on the discussion taking place in the team around the general team dream or vision and only go into a more detailed description of the desired future in a second step.

By the way, we are not talking here about the well-known SMART objective agreement method (SMART = specific, measurable, ambitious, realistic, and time-based), as is common in many organizations, but about the description of a desired, ideal image of the future, which has a high appeal for the entire team. This is the cornerstone of the entire Reteaming process. The image of the desired future should naturally look positive, that is, a positive state should be described and not the absence of something (no negation; "go to" rather than "away from"). For this purpose, we establish a so-called "as if frame": "Let us imagine for a few minutes that the team has already achieved its desired future …"

- What exactly does that look like then?
- What does the team do differently than today?
- What do the individual team members do?
- What will determine that you have reached the preferred future?
- How does it feel to be part of this team?
- What is the best thing about having achieved the vision?
- How do others react to the team?
- What has the team achieved for itself through reaching this desired future?
- What skills has the team continued to develop in this future?
- What does the team stand for?

Despite all these questions regarding shaping the preferred future, it is not about formulating a SMART goal, but about the process of developing a vision from all team members for the whole team. It is about creating an attractive "story" about the team's future. The positive orientation and the motivating effect of this vision are essential. A hasty detailing of the vision in the direction of a SMART goal would be an excessive demand for most teams at this point and would quickly bring the team dynamics into troubled waters. The desired future lives here from the desire created by the shared vision.

> **Example**
>
> "What exactly does "Motto XY" mean to you as a team? I would like to ask you to think about the future. Imagine that your best hopes regarding this workshop have been fulfilled, that the motto has become daily practice and that you are completely satisfied with yourself, the team, and the work. What exactly does this future look like? What is different now compared to today? What else? How would you describe what makes the team so special to someone you know who doesn't work in the same organization as you? What else? If you can think of things that shouldn't happen any longer, now think about what will happen instead. Describe how it feels to have arrived at the preferred future, how you are behaving, how the team is behaving, and what makes it special to be successful as a team in that future.
>
> Please take a moment, moderation cards and pens. Write down all the important aspects of your future image on one card each and hang them on the pinboard.
>
> *Variation:* Please take the wax crayons and go to the pinboard paper on the table. Draw a picture of this desirable future. It doesn't have to be a work of art. Draw together what you want and how you want to work together, so that we then have a shared vision of your preferred future as a team. Take half an hour to do this. ...
>
> Thank you very much! What do I see in your picture? Can you please describe and explain it to me?"

Once the collection of aspects of the desired team future is complete, it is summarized together in the plenum. The goal is not to obtain a complete and formulated description of the preferred future. We don't need a carefully formulated statement in the sense of a corporate vision that is used in company presentations. It should rather be an idea about the common direction of the team. Therefore, a collection of attractive aspects of the preferred future will do perfectly for the moment. By presenting the aspects in the plenum, a discussion about the common direction of the team is stimulated. Add important elements from the discussion on the pinboard. Similarly, the jointly designed picture of the desired future can be discussed in plenum and supplemented if necessary. At the end of this first step, there should be an initial, common idea of the preferred future of the team!

The difference to a problem-focused workshop becomes clear once again for everyone at this point. In many workshops, we would have a collection of problems on the pinboard at this point, which would now be sorted, summarized, and prioritized. This procedure would start the downplaying of one's own mistakes and emphasizing of the mistakes made by others. This doesn't happen in the Reteaming workshop, because we have already established a common vision (future dream) as a starting point for further work.

Yes, But...
Stimulating and accompanying a team through these questions about their own desired future and then agreeing on a vision sounds easier than it sometimes is. Quite often, when a team has decided to take part in such a team coaching, there are often negative drivers behind this decision, so that they are not in the mood yet to look for a common picture of their preferred future. Of course, the positive workshop introduction, the explanation of the workshop philosophy and the process guidance given by the coach helps. At the same time, this is no guarantee that the team will engage in this unfamiliar path. Particularly in teams, there is a danger that the group dynamics can turn against the team coach when the coach insists on talking only about the desired future and not the problematic past. Therefore, as a coach, it is important here to be clear in one's solution-focused attitude and not to go back to problem analysis ("What do you think are the causes of your problems?") at the first obstacle on the solution-focused path, but to deal with the situation creatively and flexibly. Fortunately, there is a tried-and-true entry point for such situations that some teams find easier. This possible variant is called problem transformation.

Variation "Problem Transformation"
This way is particular suitable for teams that suffer from a kind of blockade of thought when they are asked to think about the future freely and to develop a positive common vision. For example, teams that decide collectively to go on an extended coffee break when they are asked to draw a picture on the pinboard about their team vision. Or teams that see it as an indisputable truth that you must deal with the problem to make

something better. To pick up and motivate these teams as well, without getting caught up in a typical problem analysis, you can make it clear that every problem is just the flip side of a goal. This can be illustrated with the following flip chart and

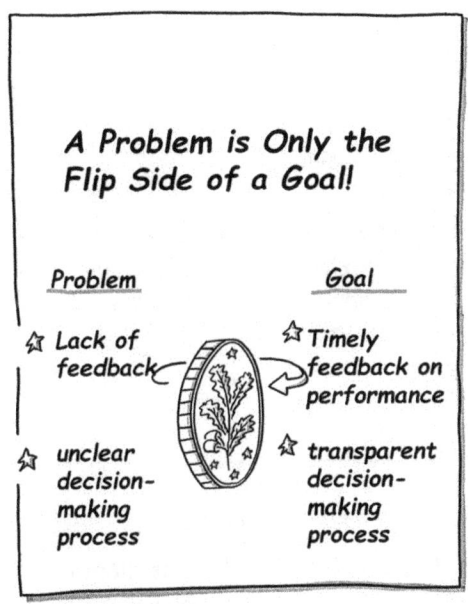

Flip chart: Problems are the flip sides of goals

a few examples that are easy for each team member to follow. To do this, another flip chart page is divided into two columns with the headings "Problem" and "Goal," respectively. On the problem side, two or three examples are written such as "lack of information flow, non-transparent decision making, or ineffective meetings." Then each problem is translated into a goal: "Optimal information flow," "Transparent decision making" or "Effective meetings."

Problem ⬇	Goal 🎯
o old computers	o modern office equipment
o lack of feedback	o timely feedback on performance
o often negative communication	o respectful communication

Flip chart: Transforming problems into goals

For a team of 12, you would ideally split them into two teams of distribute six, giving each team its own flipchart. With six people, everyone has a chance to participate in the discussion, and we have a sufficiently large diversity of perspectives. So, we need one flip chart with the prepared columns for each team of six. Even at this point, it is not yet necessary to think of a SMART description of the goal. It is perfectly adequate to simply emphasize the goal side of the issue so that the group doesn't fall into the vicious circle of problem focus, but can concentrate on the joint achievement of the goal.

For this variant, it is particularly important to refer once again to the motto of the workshop, which focuses on the team. It is therefore not a question here of recording every possible problem of the organization, but rather of possible problems that relate to the cooperation within the team. The issues must therefore be within the team's sphere of influence so that they can be successfully addressed by the team. Otherwise, it is quite tempting to write down things like "too much work" on the problem side and "hire more people" on the goal side. However, nothing would be gained by doing so, since one has only cleverly found the "scapegoat" outside the team. This example contains another temptation, which is to not write down the goal side of the problem, but to define an action with the problem in mind. This way we would get close to a normal problem-focused workshop, which is not our intention. Instead, we want to create an awareness of what we are aiming for. So, this is not about what measures to take, but about formulating the "what instead" on a problem description. Of course, we will get to the agreement of measures, but before that there is still some way to go. If you want to be fast, go slowly …

Once the idea that a problem is the flip side of a goal is understood, the group is given the following task:

> **Example**
>
> "Please form a group of about six people and gather at a flip chart. Each flip chart has a table with the column heading "Problem" and a column heading "Goal." Now, as a group, please collect all the problems that seem important to you in relation to your team and the motto of our workshop and write them in keywords in the left-hand column (problem side). Do not leave anything out and please write everything down which is related to our workshop motto. For each problem you have written down, please write directly in the right-hand column the corresponding goal. Please make sure that the goal is worded positively. For example, "transparency" instead of "not non-transparent." Please also make sure that the goal formulation is understandable without having to look at the "problem column." So, for example, instead of "should be improved, "use a concrete description like "good time management in meetings." You have 20 minutes for this task."

After about 20 minutes, most groups are finished, but of course it can also be 30 minutes. It is important that all relevant problems have been put on paper and transformed into goals. As a coach, you support the groups at the flip charts:

- ... write down all the issues (problems) related to the motto. "What else? What else? What else?"
- ... turn every single problem into a goal.
- ... to formulate the goals in a positive way, ask: "What instead?"
- ... formulate the goals in such a way that they are understandable even without knowledge of the problem.

Often the groups already find out in the process that it is much more helpful to talk about goals instead of problems. Then they often write down the goals directly and discuss how the appropriate problem might be titled. At this point, feel free to encourage the groups to focus on the goals and leave the problem column blank at this point, since we will only be working with the goals anyway.

When all groups are finished, give each group a pair of scissors and ask group members to cut the flip chart paper in half so that the problem and goal columns are separate. Now collect all the problem lists and hang all the goal collection side by side on a pinboard. Once all participants are back in the plenum, take the problem lists and—if you wish—a briefcase in which to carefully stow away the collection of problems.

> **Example**
>
> "As I mentioned at the beginning of our workshop, we will essentially deal here with your ideas for the future and not with a possible problem analysis. Therefore, we can now stow away your problems. For this purpose, I have brought my briefcase here. It is already fairly full of the problems of other teams and now your problems will be added. If you want your problems back later on, just let me know. But so far, that hasn't ever happened! And if you ever run out of problems, let me know, too. Then you are welcome to take on some of the problems that other teams have already collected and solved. But we will keep working with your goals for now!"

With this little show interlude, the topic of problem and problem analysis is usually finally concluded, and we can devote ourselves entirely to defining the goals for the rest of the workshop. However, we have modified the visioning step a little and have gone straight to a more concrete level, the level of goals. Goals are often more pragmatic than visions, but they are also often less motivating, so the preferred option should be classic visioning. Jumping directly to the level of goals stems from an understanding of the need to pick up a specific team where they are at that moment.

> **Attention**
>
> Make sure that the flip charts are cut up by a team member. After all, it is their work product, so it would be inappropriate for you to cut up your participants' flip charts. It is important to be respectful of the problem sets. Even if we don't continue to work with the team's problems, many team members may have developed a strong attachment to the team's view of its problems. Consequently, it would be insensitive if the problems simply ended up crumpled up in a waste basket.
> As a result of this phase, we now have a long list of goals to work with.

8.2   Our Goal

Every vision must be broken down into more concrete goals so that the vision can be achieved. If, up until now, we have given little or no thought to what is necessary to achieve the vision, it is now a matter of considering what goals we need to achieve on the way to vision fulfillment. Goals in this sense are milestones on the way to the desired future. It may be that the team needs to change its communication, build new competencies, or focus on new areas of responsibility to make that future a reality. Likewise, there are certain goals that I must achieve before I can reach my preferred future.

Goals divide the path to the preferred future into more concrete and easily achievable stages. What all goals have in common, therefore, is that they must contribute to the vision that was jointly described in the first step. The question at hand is: What goals do we need to achieve to get closer to our dream future? You can arrive at this list of meaningful goals in several ways, of course. You can make a list by shout-outs from the plenum, have moderation cards describe them, or discuss them in plenary and record the outcome of the discussion.

The method we use most often is called "side-talk-teams." For this, participants remain seated where they are in the circle of chairs and form small side-talk-teams with their immediate neighbors. In these small groups of two to three team members, meaningful goals are discussed and then written down on facilitation cards. With this approach, we have ensured, on the one hand, that every person participates, and at the same time, we have a larger number of meaningful goals. Side-talk-teams also help to incorporate the opinions of team members who might not speak up in a plenary session. In addition, the quality of the list of goals usually increases because the goals have already been critically discussed in the dialogue.

If we now have a list of goals, either by collecting meaningful goals with a view to the vision or by the process of problem transformation, it is a matter of selecting *the one goal* with which our work is to continue. So here both variants described in the first step come together again: in a list of goals that are important for the team. Selecting one goal from this list is not an easy task, since all goals were named by participants because they are important to them. Focusing is therefore done in several steps. The first step is to see whether there are any goals among the many that belong together in terms of content. Goals that perhaps mean the same thing in similar terms. Such goals can then be summarized and written as a consolidated goal on a new sheet of flip chart paper. Usually, after this procedure, we have four to six consolidated goals that could no longer be summarized or merged together without losing something essential. What remains is the task of agreeing on a goal to start with now. We often clarify the reason for the focus with the help of a metaphor:

> **Example**
>
> "Like an ambitious mountaineer who wants to climb all the world's eight-thousanders, we naturally want to achieve all our goals. At the same time, the mountaineer can only climb one peak at a time. Similarly, it also makes sense for us to agree on a goal with which we want to start and on the achievement of which we can fully concentrate. If possible, this should be the goal that has the biggest positive effect on all other goals. It is often the case that many things change and develop in parallel as soon as we have started to work on one goal."

Flip chart: Focusing on one goal on a time

Before agreeing on the first goal, the first peak, it is helpful to agree on what will happen to the goals that are not covered in this team coaching workshop. Once it is ensured that all goals will be worked on at some point, it is usually much easier for the team to agree on a single goal to start with. Very often it is possible for the team to look at the other goals in one of their regular jour fixes or to agree that after a certain time, there will be another workshop at a later date where they can then work on more goals. Whether these goals are worked on in the jour fixe or the next workshop is often not that important. By focusing on the goal with the strongest leverage on all the other goals and on achieving the team vision, the other goals will move and change along with it. To illustrate this, we often use the metaphor of the fishing net: No matter which knot of the net you lift, all the other knots will move with it!

The final step is then to agree on the one goal that will be the basis for the further steps in the workshop. To do this, it is helpful to highlight the goals once again and write each of them down on a piece of flip chart paper as a well-formulated goal. Well-formulated in this case means that the goal can be formulated in a concise sentence, if possible, and describes positively a state in the future (i.e., no actions or negations).

> **Attention**
>
> Sometimes the step of agreeing on the one goal the team wants to start with is a bit difficult. After all, all the goals that have been mentioned are important and meaningful. Therefore, patience and persistence are needed here. At this point, please do not take typical facilitation shortcuts that you are familiar with from other types of workshops. So neither a simple vote nor any kind of scoring. As a result, there are always people whose point of view has not been considered. At this point we explicitly want consensus. As I said, if you proceed slowly enough and take one step at a time, as described above, you will eventually arrive at a goal that is supported by everyone.

8.3 Our Supporters

Success is a team sport and people are social beings, which is why community, social belonging and mutual support are core values for most of us. Of course, this also applies to the people in team coaching. First and foremost, all team members should be able to rely on the members of their own team to support their goal achievement. We have already tried to ensure this by the first two steps. Beyond that, however, it can make sense to look for other people in the relevant environment who can support the team in its efforts to achieve its goal. We are familiar with these considerations from project management, where one systematically conducts a stakeholder analysis to identify possible sponsors, supporters, and coalition partners. As a rule, goals of teams in organizations not only have an impact on the team itself, but also on other departments or individuals. However, at this point, we do not need to conduct a classic stakeholder analysis with the team in question.

It is more a matter of discussing in the plenum which people or other teams should know about our project so that they can adapt to our activities and, if necessary, actively support us. In addition to the effect of support, approaching possible supporters also increases our own commitment to the goal. As soon as we tell someone about our goal and even ask for support, this has an additional motivating effect on us and increases our sense of commitment. In contrast, not taking our goal seriously would trigger a kind of cognitive dissonance: "How can I not take my goal seriously or not pursue it actively when others are committed to me and my goal?"

The collection of potential supporters in the plenum is accompanied by a determination of who will address these persons or teams. After the event, it is often sufficient to inform the relevant people about the process with the help of the photo documentation from the team workshop and to ask for appropriate support. It can be helpful to think briefly about what specifically you want to say to your supporters:

- Is the formulated vision understandable?
- Can the selected goal be easily communicated?
- Can the reason for choosing the first goal be conveyed?
- What is the most hoped for support?
- Why is this support important?
- What is the desired effect of the support?
- How do supporters know that the help has arrived?
- What kind of feedback is there from the team?

As soon as we find an answer to all these questions, we can be sure as a team that the vision and the goal have arrived and are anchored in the team. The search and definition of supporters lead to a further deepening of the team process, at the end of which there is a change that brings the team closer to its desired future.

Since it is usually not possible to talk to the supporters during the workshop, but only after the workshop, the process that was initiated within the team is carried over into everyday life. Therefore, the transfer into practice is initiated, even though no concrete action points or next steps have been defined yet.

The promise to talk about the desired future and the defined goal with other people outside the team is thus an important element of change. However, looking at the helpers will still be important in the next step, which is about the benefits that are expected from the changes that have been initiated.

8.4 Our Benefit

So far, we have agreed on a common vision about our preferred future as well as a first goal (summit) we want to achieve. We have also identified potential supporters for our project. But is the whole effort worth it? Will it be worth it for me personally? This question is often not explicitly voiced in many workshops, but it may still be present in the minds of team members. In team coaching, it is important that such questions come out of the backs of people's minds and move into the public team-space to be talked about. Therefore, the goal fulfillment is now reviewed with a view to the benefits for the participants.

In the previous steps, we have already considered that the vision and the jointly supported goal are meaningful for the team. In this step, we therefore first check whether the achievement of the defined goal also benefits the individual. We deliberately focus here on the goal that we have defined as the first milestone on the way to the desired future. From now on, the vision is therefore the point of orientation in the distance (our North Star), which continues to provide direction. Concretely, however, we will continue to work with the goal that we have determined together. For this purpose, we ask each participant to write down on moderation cards what will be the benefit personally from reaching the goal. Afterwards, all cards are collected and pinned to a pin board and briefly read out.

There is no discussion of the different cards at this point, as it is not about understanding the individual aspects of the benefits, but is about visualizing the usefulness of the goal achievement for each team member. It is therefore perfectly sufficient that each individual team member knows which specific benefit is meant. It doesn't matter if we don't fully understand the buzzwords or phrases on the cards at this point. What is more important is the motivational effect on the individual team members and the team when looking at the many benefit cards on the pinboard. By visualizing many different benefits, the attractiveness of the goal is once again underlined, and the motivation to work on it is increased.

However, it doesn't stop at the individual benefit check. In the second step, the benefits for other people or groups are looked at. This can again be done with moderation cards or simply by shouting out in the plenum. At this point, it is likely that many of the supporters identified earlier will also reappear. This time not as supporters, but as beneficiaries and joint winners if we achieve our goal. This makes it easier for us to approach the potential supporters after the workshop. We offer a win-win situation: On the one hand, the team benefits from the support, and on the other hand, the success of the team will help our supporters.

In addition, it is often neighboring teams, superiors, customers, suppliers, but also one's own family or even the family dog (which is mentioned surprisingly often), who will benefit from the team's success. So, the benefit check underscores once again that our agreed upon goal is important, helpful, and meaningful. The motivation in the team to move on is further increased.

8.5 Our Progress So Far

In this phase of coaching, participants often say that they are not starting from scratch and that they do not feel as if they have not yet achieved anything as a team. As SF coaches, we are of course happy to take up this hint—even if it does not come. SFC always makes sure to strengthen the clients' self-efficacy beliefs. The easiest way we do this in team coaching is by drawing a scale from zero to ten on a flip chart. Ten is defined as the perfect achievement of the goal. At ten, we have achieved all aspects of our goal and implemented them to our complete satisfaction. Zero is simply defined as the opposite of ten. Now the team members have to determine where on the scale they see the team already today. This can again be pre-discussed through side-talk-teams or discussed directly in plenary. It is also okay if the team does not agree on a number on the scale, but there is a range from, for example, three to six. The important thing here is that the team then starts to give the examples that led them to not vote for zero. All scores above zero are indications of skills, positive routines or behaviors that are already pointing in the direction of the desired future. All these positive approaches need to be brought to light to further strengthen them.

Another way to fill the scale is to (almost) anonymously distribute sticky dots on the flip chart scale. This is a variant that activates participants and has a playful feel to it:

Example

"We have talked about the goal, about possible supporters and about the benefits that achieving the goal will have for us as a team. At times this can sound as though no progress has been made towards achieving this goal up until today, which of course is not the case. If we draw a scale on the flip chart paper where ten is complete goal achievement and zero is the opposite, where does your team stand today? To capture all the team's perspectives on this question, I would ask you to stick a dot on this scale right away. The more elements of goal fulfillment you already see today, the higher the score you give. And so that the scoring can be done at least "semi-anonymously," I will turn the flip chart around. Please come one after the other behind the flip chart and stick your point. And so that the first in the row can also score anonymously, I will now stick on three dots. Now a quick photo with the cell phone, so that I can remove my points again at the end—click—and off we go!"

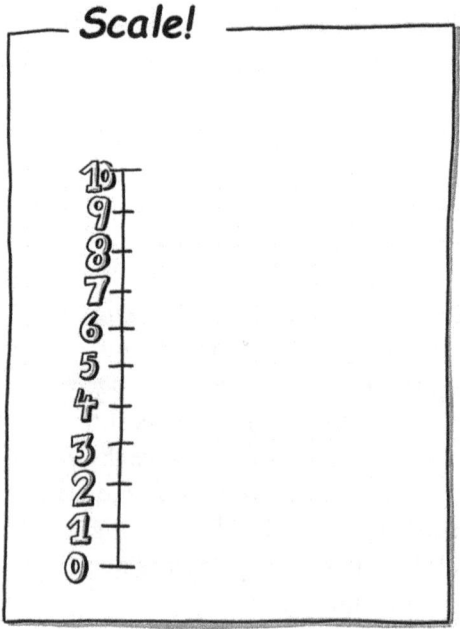

Flip chart: Where are we today regarding the goal?

After sticking the dots and removing my own dots to preserve anonymity, the resulting cloud of dots is worked with in the same way as the jointly determined scale score. The perception and emphasis of the progress made and what has been achieved so far by the group is an important step in reteaming. Once again, the aim here is to strengthen the group's self-efficacy belief, but also to further activate motivation for the next steps. As a rule, the mood in the team rises noticeably after this step!

8.6 Our Future Progress

In individual SFC, you would now ask, "How will you know that you've made a step on the scale?", so you ask for signs of progress. As you remember form the individual SFC, we deliberately do not ask what the next step would be to get a little closer to the goal. This is a difficult question for many teams and individuals to answer. It is much easier for teams or individuals to answer the question of how they will know that they are getting closer to, or have even reached, their goal. Therefore, in SFC we ask for signs of progress!

So we proceed in a similar fashion in team coaching. However, we don't refer to a specific scale value since the team has probably answered the question about the current value on the scale from zero to ten in the dot cloud done earlier. Instead, we remain more general and attempt a collective look into the future. To do this, we invite the team to an imagination exercise and assume together with the team that the goal has been achieved and that the expected benefits have also materialized, so the team has truly performed as a kind of "dream team."

- How can you tell for yourself that the team has become a dream team?
- How can the neighboring department tell that you have achieved your goals?
- How can your supporters say that you have achieved your goals?
- Over the next 4 weeks, how can you say that the team is moving toward the goal and desired future?
- By the end of the week, how can you say that the team has hit the ground running?

These and similar questions encourage the group to give as concrete a description as possible of the team after the successful changes. Often it is also helpful to talk to the team about what difference these changes make compared to today. It raises awareness that even many small changes have relevance to the team. It also increases the desire to start making changes. By describing the team as concretely as possible after the goals have been met, motivation to change grows, as does confidence in success. This is exactly what we want to achieve: An increased confidence in success and clarity about next possible steps—without asking directly about the next steps. As difficult as the question "What do you need to do next?" is for many to answer, describing what I will use to determine a small step forward when I work back from the result, i.e., the preferred future, is comparatively easy.

The signs of progress can then either be captured in key words on flip charts or creatively painted in the form of a shared picture. What also works well for many teams is to hold a press conference from the future.

> **Example**
>
> "It has been a year since the first team coaching workshop. The team has met and perhaps exceeded all its goals. As a result, the team has become known throughout the organization for its successes. To mark the occasion, you are now asked to hold a press conference in which you share the secret of your success. Please describe …
>
> - … how does the team work together today now that the goal has been achieved? What is the difference to the year before?
> - … what have been the most significant changes?
> - … what did you notice after half a year that showed you that the team coaching workshop was still having an effect?
> - … how could you tell—1 month after the team coaching workshop—that the changes were moving in the right direction?
> - what were the first signs after the team workshop that something had changed?
> - … what convinced even die-hard skeptics that the team was developing successfully?
> - … what advice do you have for other teams to achieve similar success?"

This gives you a description of a preferred future that already contains all the elements that can be addressed in the coming days and weeks. If the signs of progress are then put into a logical and chronological order, you get, quite incidentally, a possible plan for the next few weeks. Of course, this plan may still change in practice. It is even likely that it will still be flexibly adapted to the respective situation and its development. Nevertheless, the collection of signs of progress designs a kind of master plan for the next few weeks that can be used as a guide and motivation again and again.

8.7 Our Challenges

With all the focus on solutions and all the talk about the desired future, there should never be the feeling that the current gravity of the situation is not being taken seriously. Therefore, in Reteaming, there is explicit space to acknowledge the challenges the team is facing. This is a distinctive feature of Reteaming that does not necessarily exist in other forms of SF Coaching. Again, though, it is important not to start with the challenges in team coaching, but to emphasize the solution-focused perspective at the beginning. It makes a big difference whether I start with the vision, the goal, the supporters, past successes, and the dream team and then talk about possible challenges or whether I start with the challenges. It is like a pair of glasses that I put on at the beginning of the team coaching and through which I look at all the further steps.

We are now at the point where we know what we want our future to look like and that we will see progress towards the preferred future. Now we also need to pick up the skeptics in the team and acknowledge that these changes will not happen by themselves. The easiest way to do this is to talk about it in plenum. It often makes sense to prepare the plenary exchange with a short side-talk-team session, so that even the more hesitant voices can be heard. After all, that is what it is all about: all voices should be heard.

After the plenary discussion, summary key words on the various challenges can be written on flip charts. As a rule, we deliberately keep the visualization of the challenges brief, as they should not take up too much space in purely visual terms. Nevertheless, they must be recorded to document respect for the challenges. Ultimately, naming the difficulties and challenges is an essential preparation for looking at the resources in the team. If something is difficult, it implicitly means that it is possible. Otherwise it would not be "difficult" to achieve, but simply impossible. In this way, we use the collected challenges directly for the next step in Reteaming: strengthening confidence in success!

8.8 Our Confidence

Strengthening confidence in success is of course particularly important now because we don't want to simply leave the challenges hanging in the air. The challenges make it clear to us that achieving our goals may not be easy, but also reinforce the fact that, above all, it will be possible. To do so, we simply must overcome the challenges. This is an ideal opportunity, once again, for teams to become aware of the strengths, competencies, and accumulated experience within the team. So now it's time to gather the reasons why the team will be successful. To do this, write a question on a flip chart and have participants write their answers on moderation cards. The question is:

> "What gives you the confidence that you are capable of achieving your goal?"

Deepen this step by encouraging the side-talk-teams to think about competencies and skills that have been necessary to be successful as a team so far by asking the following questions on a flip chart.

- How have we managed to deal with challenges in the past?
- What competencies and skills were/are required for this?
- Which competencies of the team are particularly valued by outsiders?
- What characterizes the team in general? What are our strengths?
- How have we managed to achieve success so far?
- What else?

These questions don't all have to be answered individually, but should only serve as suggestions to write strengths, competencies, skills, and all other resources of the team as bullet points on moderation cards. Once all cards have been written, the cards are hung on a pin board and viewed together in the plenum. Like the individual benefits, promoting motivation and confidence in success is an important element for the further course of the workshop.

At this point, you can also recall the introductory exercise ("Getting to know each other—somehow different"), in which resources were named for each team member that can be helpful for the success of the team coaching. It quickly becomes clear that the number of resource cards far exceeds the number of challenges. Of course, this is first a quantitative impression. Nevertheless, such "images" are important for strengthening the feeling of self-efficacy and thus confidence in success.

To add to the confidence, the plenary can then collect resources on the flip charts that are outside the team but can be helpful for team success. These include, of course, supporter resources, collaborations with other teams, shared goals with other parts of the organization, and much more.

8.9 Our Promise

A promise is about both a commitment you make to another person and a public confirmation of your intention to honor that commitment. Both are to ensure that something gets done, and that is where we are now in the Reteaming process. After all, it is nice that we have defined a goal as well as the confidence to achieve it. However, nothing will happen if no one acts. Therefore, team members are asked to make a promise about what will be done in the near future to bring the team closer to its goal. It is simply a matter of following up the team coaching with concrete actions.

Since we are all too familiar from psychology with the phenomenon of diffusion of responsibility in groups (one of the others will do it), it is now a matter of everyone considering what he or she will do in the next few days or 2 weeks at the most so that the signs of progress already discussed also show up in practice. So we are back to the signs of the desired future. This time, however, not with the pure description, but with the actions that make these signs a reality. There should be an emphasis on steps that are as concrete as possible and as small as possible. Therefore, it also helps to set the time horizon to somewhere between the next few days up to a maximum of 2 weeks to ensure that the plans are also implemented. The smaller these steps are, the simpler the actions are, the higher the probability that they will also be implemented in everyday life.

This way we use the motivation for change built throughout the workshop (vision, goal, supporters, benefits, progress to date, signs of progress, challenges, and confidence in success) to make the smallest possible steps to start the change momentum a reality. The positive tension and anticipation have been built-up over the course of the workshop, so that team motivation, as well as confidence in success, is such that everyone wants to do their part to achieve the desired future.

In concrete terms, the participants in the team coaching are asked to consider, either individually or in tandems, what they will do to ensure that the changes are implemented successfully. Sometimes it can also make sense to give this task to small working groups rather than to individual team members. This is always useful if subgroups of the team are needed for the upcoming changes.

Now you can incorporate a short reflection walk. The participants of the team coaching workshop have worked very intensively so far, so it is advisable to move around and reflect on the status of the deliberations with a little distance. To do this, ask participants to go for a short walk of 20 minutes in groups of two or three and talk about the goal, the preferred future, and their personal promises. Such a walk helps team members to choose and cement their individual promise even more consciously and to receive immediate feedback from one or two colleagues about the impact on the goal. After the walk, all participants come back to the plenum and share their promise with the team. This virtually guarantees change towards the preferred future through everyone's promise of change.

In conclusion to this step, all promises can be recorded on a pin board including names. In this way, without having used the word, you automatically arrive at a kind of action plan for the next 2 weeks, which can then also be reviewed at a next meeting.

8.10 Our Progress Monitoring

For most team workshops, this would probably be the end of the team intervention. After all, you have a goal and several concrete actions that will bring you closer to that goal. With team coaching à la Reteaming, this is actually where the work really begins. After all, it is not just about a successful workshop, but above all about consolidating the "new" view of the team and delivering on the promises made.

It is important to maintain a resource perspective for the team and to integrate appreciation for the other team members even more strongly into everyday life. This is expressed in the implementation of the Reteaming philosophy: "No one is (solely) responsible for the problem, but everyone is responsible for the solution!" It is important to emphasize and stress this point of view again and again in the subsequent meetings.

The team lead has a special role to play here. Leaders lead primarily by example. It is therefore particularly important for the success of the team coaching that the team lead focuses on the small steps = successes in the direction of the goal in the coming days and weeks. Of course, there will be things that happen that don't contribute towards achieving the goal. The challenge for the team lead now is to overlook some of the things that are not going as agreed, and instead see all the things that are going well. By continuously reinforcing the behaviors that are desirable and helpful, these behaviors automatically become more frequent. This effect is, of course, on the one hand, a classic reinforcement of desired behaviors. On the other hand, it is also a systematic change in the team culture. In the team coaching workshop itself, it is important to emphasize the importance of progress monitoring once again and to make everyone aware of it. To deepen this awareness, side-talk-teams can be used to collect possibilities of how progress monitoring can be established in everyday life. Typical examples that are mentioned include:

- At least once a week, tell every colleague what you were happy about in terms of their behavior or work.
- Progress wall: visualization of promises kept, actions taken, and everything that has happened that supports the goal.

- Positive feedback round at the end of jour fixe meetings.
- Daily stand-up meeting on goals for the day, including finding ways to support each other.

Particularly the various possibilities for constant visualization of progress today fit very well into the agile work of teams that are already used to Kanban or task boards, which are viewed and completed in daily stand ups. At this point, a column on these or similar boards can be reserved for progress. Weekly retrospectives, which also focus on the team's progress, also fit in with this. This doesn't just mean discussing progress towards the preferred future that was agreed upon at the workshop. Rather, it is also important to become more sensitive to progress of a general nature within the team. As we have already emphasized, the fishing net metaphor applies to changes also in the direction of the desired future: as soon as you lift one knot of the net, other knots will also move. Similarly, progress in the team will be seen in places that were not planned or imagined at all. These positive changes also need to be noticed and strengthened.

> **Attention!**
> Monitoring progress and reinforcing positive approaches does not mean that we can no longer talk about problems, difficulties, and challenges. However, the way problems are dealt with will be different. If there are difficulties in the team, the first reflex should no longer be to ask: "Who is responsible for this?", but "What do we want instead?". As explained above, the problem and the goal are each two sides of the same coin. Which side of the coin we look at more intensively and energize is up to us.

8.11 Our Strategies Against Setbacks

This point is also missing in most team workshops: How do we deal with setbacks in our efforts to change? Of course, Reteaming is focused on the preferred future, but it is not positive thinking in the sense of "if we just believe it, it will happen." Reteaming is born out of practice and therefore knows that there is no change in life without setbacks. These do not have to be major, but it is likely that there will be moments in team life that

8 It Is Only 12 Steps: The Team Coaching Workshop

are negative to the vision, the team future, or the promises made. If you suppress this thought in team coaching, these setbacks hit all the harder when they do occur. To prevent this, one collects with the team (if necessary, also in small groups of six members) on a flip chart paper all obstacles and possible setbacks, which could occur on the way to the desired future. The flip chart page is structured like the problem transformation flip chart page:

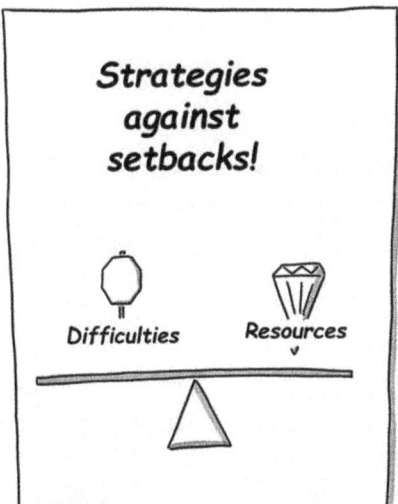

Flip charts: Strategies against setbacks

The left-hand column lists all possible obstacles and setbacks. The column on the right lists all the resources and strategies that will be used to counter these specific obstacles and possible setbacks. The more concrete the counter strategies for a specific obstacle, the more helpful they will be. Encourage teams to look for resources among team members, as well as among supporters and outside the team. Here, you can build on the results and findings from steps three, "Our Supporters," and eight, "Our Confidence."

One item that came up on every obstacle list I have seen so far was *"time,"* or the lack of it. The important thing here is that you trust the team to find the countermeasures that are appropriate for the team. The point here is not to bring in the ideal strategy from the latest time management system, but to find the strategy that best fits the reality of the team. What that is, only the team knows. Overall, this step should not take too long. Most groups take around 20 minutes to collect the likely setbacks and list the counter strategies. Very often, the counter strategies are also repetitive, as it often involves refocusing, leveraging existing resources inside and outside the team, and constantly recalibrating priorities for the team. Ultimately, it is important for participants to be aware that unexpected events can occur and to have the resources to deal with them flexibly and get back on track towards a preferred future.

8.12 Our Celebration of Successes

Of course, it is also important to celebrate successes! The team has set out on its journey and will move closer to the desired future step by step. In this context, it is helpful for the general motivation and the perseverance that successes are celebrated. These can be large and small milestones, but also unplanned positive changes or simply the realization that the team is on the right track. Supporters outside the team are also happy when they can celebrate successes of the team they have supported. If one feels part of a team, whether as a member or an external supporter, team successes are an important source of positive social identity. This positive social identity, in turn, fosters team spirit and a willingness to work hard for the team. The team becomes a source of satisfaction and joy—not always, but more and more often. Rituals such as the solution-focused retrospective at the end of a work week also help, so that even the small steps towards a desired future can be celebrated. Even if you never end up doing a solution-focused team coaching workshop, you might still take this one point and make sure your team regularly celebrates its successes!

Conclusion and Review
With the steps "progress monitoring" and "celebrating successes," we have already left the workshop and entered the transfer to daily life. At this point, the question arises as to how team coaching should be

continued beyond the 12 steps of Reteaming. There are now various possibilities for this, some of which can also be combined:

- Arrangement of another workshop to work on further goals.
- Arrangement of a review workshop to ensure success.
- Debriefing of the workshop by the team lead and coach.
- Accompanying coaching of the team lead as a key promoter of the initiated change process in everyday life.
- Accompanying coaching of the team within the framework of team meetings daily.

However, in SFC we assume that the above-mentioned activities are not absolutely necessary. Of course, these forms of further support can be expressed as a wish by the team or the team lead. However, we assume that the team will do what seems to make sense for the team in the current situation, independently of external input. A basic assumption of our work is that our clients have all the resources to make their lives better. In team coaching, they have now decided on the goal and the first steps to do this. In addition, we still assume that change will happen no matter what. Team coaching simply supports the team in directing the changes towards the preferred future. We trust the team to find its way. Should it need further support in the form of Reteaming, it will know how to contact the SF Coach.

To end the current team coaching, a follow-up discussion with the team lead is therefore usually sufficient and has a certain elegance, as the process was also started with such a two-way discussion. This final meeting, therefore, provides a well-rounded closure to the process, with the team well on the way to its preferred future, all based on a single, well-run SF workshop.

In this spirit, I wish all readers success and joy with your first solution focused Reteaming Workshop!

Jörg Middendorf

Literature

Asay und Lambert in "The Heart and Soul of Change" (1999), Eds. A. Hubble et al., American Psychological Association

Bamberger G. G. (2015, 5th edition, first edition 1999) Lösungsorientierte Beratung, Beltz Verlag, Weinheim

Bandura A. (1977) Self-Efficacy: Toward a Unifying Theory of Behavioral Change. In: Psychological Review. 84 (2)

Bannink F. (2015) Lösungsfokussierte Fragen: Handbuch für die lösungsfokussierte Gesprächsführung, Hogrefe Verlag, Göttingen (Original edition 2006 Oplossingsgerichte vragen. Handboek oplossingsgerichte gespreksvoering, Pearson Assessment and Information, Amsterdam)

De Jong, P. und Kim Berg, I. (1998) Lösungen (er)finden: Das Werkstattbuch der lösungsorientierten Kurzzeittherapie, Verlag Modernes Leben, Dortmund

De Shazer S. (1994) Words were originally magic, W.W. Norton & Company, New York

De Shazer S. (1985) Keys to Solution in Brief Therapy, W. W. Norton & Company, New York

De Shazer S. (1988) Clues, Investigating Solutions in Brief Therapy, W. W. Norton & Company, New York

De Shazer S. (1991) Putting Difference to Work, W.W. Norton & Company, New York

De Shazer S. und Dolan Y. (2007) More than Miracles, Routledge London

Literature

Iveson C., George E., Ratner H. (2012a) Brief Coaching: A Solution Focused Approach, Routledge, London

Kim Berg I. Student's Corner http://www.sfbta.org/BFTC/Steve&Insoo_PDFs/insoo_students_corner.pdf; Zugriff 2017-01-27

Kim Berg I. Paradigm-Shift http://www.sfbta.org/BFTC/Steve&Insoo_PDFs/paradigm-shift.pdf;Zugriff 2017-01-27

Meier D. und Szabó P. (2008a) Coaching erfrischend anders, Solutions Surfers GmbH/Weiterbildungsforum, Luzern

O'Connell B., Palmer S., Williams, H. (2014) Lösungsorientiertes Coaching in der Praxis, Junfermann Verlag Paderborn (Original edition 2012, Routledge London)

Watzlawick P. (1967) Pragmatics of Human Communication, A Study of Interactional Patterns, Pathologies, and Paradoxes; W.W. Norton & Company, New York

Furman, B. und Ahola, T. (2007): Handbook of reteaming, Helsinki Brief Therapy Institute, Helsinki

Furman, B. und Ahola, T. (2010): Es ist nie zu spät, erfolgreich zu sein: Ein lösungsfokussiertes Programm für Coaching von Organisationen, Teams und Einzelpersonen, Carl-Auer-Systeme Verlag, Heidelberg

Furman, B. und Ahola, T. (2013): Raus aus dem Tief: Übungen für mehr Lebensfreude, Carl-Auer-Systeme Verlag, Heidelberg (Original edition 2011 Palautoa elämänilosi, Tammi, Helsinki)

Geisbauer, W. (Hrsg.) (2012): Reteaming: Methodenhandbuch zur lösungsorientierten Beratung, Carl-Auer-Systeme Verlag, Heidelberg

Iveson C., George E., Ratner H. (2012b): Brief Coaching: A Solution Focused Approach, Routledge, London

Meier D. und Szabó P. (2008b): Coaching erfrischend anders, Solutions Surfers GmbH/Weiterbildungsforum Luzern

GPSR Compliance

The European Union's (EU) General Product Safety Regulation (GPSR) is a set of rules that requires consumer products to be safe and our obligations to ensure this.

If you have any concerns about our products, you can contact us on

ProductSafety@springernature.com

In case Publisher is established outside the EU, the EU authorized representative is:

Springer Nature Customer Service Center GmbH
Europaplatz 3
69115 Heidelberg, Germany

www.ingramcontent.com/pod-product-compliance
Lightning Source LLC
LaVergne TN
LVHW041204250326
834689LV00001BA/5